Overcoming Social Anxiety

How to Be Yourself and How to Stop Being Afraid of Social Interaction

Jennifer Butler Green

advice. The content of this book has been derived from various sources. Please consult a licensed professional before attempting any techniques outlined in this book.

By reading this document, the reader agrees that under no circumstances are is the author responsible for any losses, direct or indirect, which are incurred as a result of the use of information contained within this document, including, but not limited to, —errors, omissions, or inaccuracies.

Contents

Introduction

Anxiety is a condition where one is in a troubled state of nervousness. It is a state of undesirable feelings of fear or uncertainty over the future similar to the feeling of imminent death. Anxiety is very different from fear. Fear refers to a reaction to something that is real or perceived as an immediate threat, but on the other hand, anxiety is an anticipated future threat that may not necessarily be real. Anxiety is characterized by fear and worries and is mostly termed as an overreaction to a situation that is a subjective menace. Anxiety also comes accompanied by tensions of the muscles, restlessness, and fatigue and concentration problems. Anxiety is healthy, but when it is extreme and goes on for a long period, it may result to an anxiety disorder.

People who suffer from anxiety show withdrawal symptoms from situations that have triggered anxiety in their past. There are several varieties of anxiety when someone experiences angst or nihilistic feelings. Other varieties of anxiety include stranger anxiety as well as social anxiety. This book will concentrate on social anxiety; however, it is good to have a comprehensive understanding of anxiety in general before we delve into social anxiety. Social anxiety happens when someone is fearful and anxious around unfamiliar people or even other people that he or she is used to.

Anxiety can occur for a short period or extend for a lengthy span. Anxiety disorders are among a group of mental disorders defined by feelings of being anxious and fearful, while the trait anxiety is about worrying about future events. Disorders related to anxiety could be genetic but may also arise due to drug use as well as withdrawal from drugs. Anxiety is associated with other mental disorders, such as bipolar condition, personality disorders, and others related to eating. Common choices for treatment include lifestyle changes, visiting a therapist, and medication.

Anxiety occurs in situations that seem unavoidable, but in reality, they are. Signs of anxiety differ in number, strength, and the rate at which they occur depending on the particular person. Almost every person has had an experience with anxiety at a certain point in their lives even though a majority do not develop long-term problems related to anxiety. Anxiety that is caused by the need to select between two options that are the same is a common issue for individuals and organizations. Currently, everyone is faced with greater choices, and competition is also stiff while there is limited time to consider options or seek advice.

When it comes to making up one's mind, not knowing what to expect, the fear of the unknown can spark emotional explosions in anxiety patients and this negatively influences the process of making decisions. This kind of anxiety disorder is divided into two types.

The first one is a choice that has multiple probable outcomes with known probabilities, while the second one is the uncertainty as well as ambiguity related to a decision where there are multiple possible outcomes with unknown probabilities.

Let me share with you my own personal story. Maybe some of the thoughts I had are also familiar to you. Some of them were as follows:

- I could not get my thoughts from spinning round and round.

- I used to wake up with a feeling of dread, and I had no idea why.

- I could also not stop worrying about my kids, whether they are doing fine, and asking myself if I was doing enough to assist them.

My worries involved thoughts about negative events that might occur in the future or sometimes about things that I had done or said in the past that I wish I could have tackled differently. Additionally, I also had concerns about what other people thought about my actions. Some of the questions and concerns I raised when I first visited a specialist were as follows:

- What was I to do to feel less stressed, angry, and overwhelmed?

- What was I to do if I felt panicky?

- What was I to do to stop worrying about everything?

Eventually, I got help, and that is why I am writing this book to assist other people that are in the same predicament that I experienced. I hope that this book will be helpful. My purpose is to help people like you overcome social anxiety, and by picking up this book, you have made the first bold step to recovery. This book is a one-stop shop for everything you would want to know about social anxiety.

Are you happy with your life right now? What would make you happy? Do you have a plan for getting it? Would you like some help? I might be able to help you. Are you be interested? Sign up for my newsletter. I give out a free workbook to help with social anxiety issues so those who sign up. I am also writing more books and posting articles that can help deal with other issues related to social anxiety. There's also a community that I'm building for people who are going through similar issues as you. If it's okay with you, I'd also like to get your feedback so I can write more about things that could help you. Does that sound like something that might help you? I hope it does, because I really want to help. I have been in your shoes before so I know how it feels. Join my newsletter and let's all help each other. Does that sound good? Visit my website now at **http://jen.green** and join my newsletter!

Chapter One:

Understanding Social

Anxiety

Social anxiety refers to the great and intense fear of social situations that causes a huge problem in one's life. It is triggered by situations that are defined as social. Social situations include parties, lunches, dates, presentations, speeches, or even exams. Those who suffer from social anxiety tend to feel as if they will be negatively judged by others and that they will suffer from humiliation or extreme embarrassment. At times, a person may feel extreme anxiety up to a point that it escalates into a full-blown panic attack. Individuals who suffer from anxiety know that their fear is irrational, but they can't do anything to stop it.

Now that you know what social anxiety is, let me tell you what it's not. Social anxiety is not just a feeling of shyness, nervousness, or the fear of talking to strangers. In the event that most of the times you become unreasonably filled with anxiety during social interactions but you feel a sigh of relief when you are not with others, then chances are that you are suffering from social anxiety. Social anxiety disorder was earlier known as social phobia and is a much greater problem than past estimates projected. A lot of people all over the world suffer from social anxiety.

In America, studies and extensive research have ranked social anxiety disorder as number 3. It follows depression and alcoholism. It is estimated that approximately slightly less than 10 percent of the population in the United States suffers from some form of social anxiety. Additionally, the prevalence rate within one's lifespan for developing social anxiety disorder is at an average of 13.5 percent. A social anxiety disorder that is specific is when a person is afraid of talking specifically in front of a group of people. On the other hand, when a person suffers from generalized social anxiety disorder, he or she is always full of anxiety, nervousness, and uneasiness in almost each and every social interaction.

It is more likely for individuals with social anxiety disorder to have a generalized kind of this disorder. When anticipatory anxiety, depression, worry, and inferiority feelings among others cut across most situations in life, a generalized type of social anxiety is involved.

Symptoms of Social Anxiety

Those who suffer from social anxiety disorder experience major emotional distress when in situations such as the following:

- getting to be introduced to other people

- being criticized and teased

- being the center of attention

- when being watched while doing an activity

- meeting individuals who are in authority

- most social interactions, especially when in the company of strangers

- moving around a room and having to talk

- friendship or romantic interpersonal relations

The psychological symptoms associated with social anxiety disorder may include intense fear, increased heartbeat, blushing, increased sweating, dryness of the throat and mouth, and trembling among others. The most common feature, however, is a constant and intense anxiety that doesn't fade away. On the other hand, socially anxious individuals face their everyday fears.

It is important to know that only adequate and appropriate treatment works to get rid of social anxiety disorder even though very few people have any knowledge of it.

Social Anxiety Disorder in Kids

This disorder can also be detected in kids. Some of the symptoms of social anxiety disorder in kids are as follows:

- frequent tantrums and cries

- having frequent tantrums

- avoiding interactions with other children and adults

- being afraid of classroom activities, performances, and social events

- avoiding asking for help from other students

- being very dependent on their parents or caregivers

Consult your general physician just in case if you're worried about your kid. Your doctor will ask you about your child's problems and talk to them about their feelings. Social anxiety treatments in children are similar to those for adults and teenagers even though medication isn't normally used. Therapy will be customized to your kid's age, and most of the time, it will involve your assistance. You can also be provided with training as well as self-help kits to use in between the sessions. It may also take place in a little group.

Have you been extremely afraid of getting judged by others? Do you tend to be very self-conscious in social interactions each passing day? Do you find it difficult interacting with unfamiliar people? In case you have felt this way for several months and these feelings make it difficult for you to carry out your day-to-day duties, such as talking to individuals at work or school, then you may have a social anxiety disorder. Social anxiety disorder, which is also referred to as social phobia, is a health condition that affects us mentally. It is a major, recurring fear of being watched and judged by other people. This fear can affect your work, school, and any other day-to-day activities. It can even make it harder for you to make and keep friends. However, social anxiety disorder doesn't have to stop you from reaching your full potential. Treatment can help you overcome your symptoms.

How does one feel when suffering from social anxiety disorder?

While in school, I was always afraid of being called on even when I knew the answers. I never wanted individuals to think I was stupid or boring. My heartbeat would race, and I would also feel lightheaded and sick. When I got a job, I always hated meeting with my boss or talking in a meeting. I couldn't even attend my best friend's wedding reception because I was afraid of having to meet new people. I also tried calming myself down by drinking several glasses of wine before events, and then I started to go out and drink every day so I could face what I had to do.

I finally had to talk to my doctor because I used to be exhausted of feeling this way, far from being worried that I would lose my job. I considered getting on medication and meeting a counselor to speak about ways of coping with my fears. I quit taking alcohol as a way of escaping from my fears.

What Is Social Panic Disorder?

Social anxiety condition is a common kind of anxiety disorder. An individual with social anxiety condition feels symptoms of panic or fear in specific or all social circumstances—for example, meeting new individuals, dating, being on the job interview, answering something in class, or needing to talk to a cashier within a store. Doing daily things in front of people, such as eating, drinking in front of others, or even using an open public restroom, also causes anxiety and fear. The person is usually afraid that she or he will end up being humiliated, judged, and turned down.

The fear that men and women with social anxiety condition have in social conditions is really strong that they will feel it up to a point that it will be beyond their control. People with social anxiety disorder might worry about things for days before they happen if they actually will. Occasionally, they end up avoiding places or even events where they believe they might do something that may embarrass them.

Some men and women with the disorder may not have anxiety within social functions but have got performance anxiety instead. They will feel physical symptoms associated with panic in situations where they have to give a speech, play a game, dance, or play a musical instrument on stage. Interpersonal anxiety disorder is not really unusual; research suggests that about 7 percent of American citizens are affected. Without therapy, social anxiety disorder may last for many years or even a lifetime and prevent a person from achieving his or her optimum potential.

What Can Cause Social Anxiety Disorder?

Sometimes social anxiety disorder runs in families. However, nobody really has the answer as to why some members of the family are affected while others are just okay. Several research studies have revealed that many brain sections are associated with worry and anxiety. Some experts believe that misreading of others' behavior may play a role in leading to or worsening social anxiety. For instance, you may think that individuals are staring or frowning at you when, in reality, they are not. Underdeveloped social skills may also possibly contribute to one's social anxiety. For example, if a person has underdeveloped social skills, he or she may feel discouraged after talking to people and may be worried about doing it in the future. By carrying out research reading and getting more knowledge about fear and anxiety in the brain, scientists will have the ability to come up with better remedies. Experts are also looking for ways in which stress and environmental factors may play a role.

Causes of Social Anxiety

A person can have limited or selective anxiety. For instance, symptoms may only occur when you're eating in front of people or talking to other people. Symptoms can also occur in all social settings if your social anxiety disorder is extreme.

The real cause of social anxiety is not known even though some research studies reveal that it is as a result of environmental triggers and gene structures. Horrendous encounters can also contribute to this condition, including bullying, family turmoil, and sexual abuse. Physical abnormalities, like serotonin imbalance, may also lead to social anxiety. Serotonin is a brain chemical that is responsible for influencing one's feelings. If the amygdala is excessively active, our answers, feelings, and thoughts of anxiety can also cause this disorder.

Anxiety attacks can run in families. However, researchers aren't sure if they're actually connected to genetic factors. For example, children might develop panic attacks by learning the behavior of just one of their parents who has an anxiety disorder. Kids can also develop anxiety disorders due to being raised in environments that are controlling and overprotective.

Diagnosing Social Anxiety Disorder

There is no medical test for checking for social anxiety disorder. Your health-care provider is able to diagnose social phobia from the description of your symptoms. Specialists can also diagnose social phobia after certain behavioral patterns are examined. During your appointment, your health-care provider will ask you to clarify your symptoms. They will also ask you to discuss situations that cause your symptoms. The requirements for social anxiety disorder include the following:

- a continuous fear of social situations due to fear of humiliation or embarrassment

- a feeling of anxiety or panic before a social interaction

- a realization that your fears are unreasonable

- anxiety that disrupts your daily life

Genetic Reasons for Social Anxiety Disorder

Individuals with a parent or parents who've suffered from social anxiety disorder have a 30–40 percent higher chance of suffering from the disorder. However, it is not possible to determine whether the parent-child social anxiety connection is based on genes and how much is based on parenting style, which is naturally influenced by the occurrence of the disorder.

Recent research into specific genetic guns for social anxiety have centered on changes in a gene that is linked to the transportation of serotonin. Shortages and excesses of serotonin have been connected to social anxiety symptoms, and people with interpersonal anxiety disorder struggle to produce serotonin constantly. Deviation from the regular activity of serotonin is linked to social anxiety disorder. Consequently, that faulty genetics can be passed from parents to children.

Interpersonal Anxiety Disorder and the Brain

Brain scans have revealed that individuals with interpersonal anxiety disorder suffer from hyperactivity in a part of the brain known as the amygdala. Activity within the amygdala triggers a surge in symptoms linked to extreme anxiety, including a rapid heartbeat, sweaty palms, respiratory excitement, muscle tightening, an increase in blood sugar levels, and a stagnation of the brain that leaves people suffering from anxiety, unable to think or reason rationally.

When people experience an increase in anxiety, mental focus shifts to a part of the brain called the prefrontal cortex. It is the role of the prefrontal cortex to suppress those reactions by monitoring them in a rational and calm manner, and if no real threat is present, it is supposed to send signals to the amygdala that defuses its anxious response. However, in social anxiety sufferers, the prefrontal cortex actually amplifies the activity of the amygdala rather than calming it down. Guys suffering from social anxiety have quite an established and deeply rooted fear of other people's views about them to the extent that their brains interpret social interactions as acceptable red flags, and no kind of rational reasoning can adequately erase those fears.

The good news is that brains can be reprogrammed to form new circuits and connections at any age. With the help of cognitive-behavioral treatment, which is the preferred form of treatment for social anxiety, people with social anxiety disorder can rewire their brains to react more rationally and in a reflective way during social interactions that pose no real danger.

The Result of Parenting Designs on Social Anxiety

Considerable studies have confirmed a link between negative parenting styles and anxiety attacks, including interpersonal social phobia disorder. When parents control their kids too much, always criticize, rarely show love, or are always worried about what others think, a kid may grow up with similar characteristics.

Kids become more afraid and suspicious of other people when they are brought up in such an environment, and their self-esteem may be negatively affected as well. During such situations, parents never realize that their actions are harmful. Social stress disorder is usually not diagnosed until sufferers get into adulthood, but symptoms have a tendency to initially manifest in late childhood or earlier adolescence. This bolsters the idea that parental designs and behavior affect or play a formational role in the development of the disorder.

Environment Influences and Stressful Existence Experiences as a Reason for Social Anxiety

Undesirable events and trauma in one's childhood can trigger the growth of social stress issues. Some of the reasons that have been proven to have predictive value for social anxiety are the following:

- physical, sexual, or emotional mishandling

- bullying or being teased by age mates

- family wrangles, household chaos, and ending of marriages

- demise of or neglection by a parent

- maternal pressure while pregnant or during infancy

Traumatic events can reinforce the idea that the entire world is a scary and unpredictable place, and it can be especially shocking and frustrating to kids to find out that their caregivers are equipped for self-centered or hurtful behavior.

Earlier Experiences and Surroundings That Lead to Social Anxiety

There is a massive amount of research and expert testimonies that show individuals often develop social anxiety as a result of traumatic encounters and surroundings concentrated with anxiety. Social anxiety usually manifests itself during childhood or puberty. Here are some examples of encounters and environments that tend to cause social anxiety in individuals:

- too much social isolation, including studying in isolation in academic surroundings

- growing up with parents, caretakers, or guardians who are overprotective, quite controlling, restrictive, or very anxious

- horrendous bullying

- abuse emotionally, physically, sexually, and verbally

- addictions to or withdrawals from drugs

- excessive utilization of technology that does not involve in-person or face-to-face interaction

- traumatic conflicts and friction within the family, such as violence or ugly divorces

- people in their particular environment not accepting all of them or discriminating against all of them based on part associated with their identity, including lovemaking orientation, race, and religious beliefs

In order to illustrate how environments plus experiences can develop interpersonal anxiety, a therapist by the name Asta Klimaite offered an example in which a child whose moms and dads prevented him from actively playing sports because they thought he'd be horribly wounded. Simply because they were his moms and dads and he was too young to find out any better, this boy accepted their attitude because he was being reasonable and obedient. To shield himself from the dangers they explained, he avoided social scenarios and developed social panic. Caregivers can also instill interpersonal anxiety in their kids by negatively framing interpersonal opportunities as dangerous rather than positively framing them as challenging. This is according to a psychologist named Helen Odessky.

Another thinking pattern kids can learn according to Odessky is interpreting ambiguous habits in a way that will provoke anxiety. A worthless glance or gesture within a social setting may cause socially anxious men and women to ruminate on what this could mean for all of them.

Negative Beliefs and Maladaptive Behavior That Cause Interpersonal Anxiety

To protect themselves from various threats that they will perceive, men and women sometimes create a system of negative values and maladaptive behaviors that will cause social anxiety. Individuals with social anxiety are likely to have at minimum some of the following thoughts whenever ruminating on upcoming interpersonal events or situations, according to Klimaite, Smerling, and therapist John L. Clarke, who studied psychology along with the father of intellectual therapy, Aaron Beck:

- I'm going to do something embarrassing.

- I was never going to belong.

- I am not likable.

- People are going to hate me.

- I'm going to pass away.

- People will know that I am nervous.

- I don't know very well what to say.

- I possess nothing to offer.

- Nobody will want to become my friend.

- I am going to say something stupid.

- Something is wrong with me.

At times, these thoughts are attached to self-esteem. When people feel like they are not worthy, it's easy for them to believe they can't offer anything in a social situation. It isn't only fear of social criticism. They may not feel like they deserve the great things about social interactions that will certainly go well. To negate the risk of these anxieties, individuals with social anxiety avoid many relationships with others. This strategy might allow them to reduce their symptoms and make them avoid confronting their social stress, but it comes at the expense of limiting how full their lives are. It also makes it hard for them to deal with social conditions when they will need to.

Psychologically Beating Themselves Up Just before Other People Can Perform It

Doctor Friedemann Schaub, who authored *The Concern and Anxiety Solution*, offered a client's story that shows the link between the experiences, values, and behaviors that result in and keep social anxiety. When he was growing up as a child, Schaub's client had a father who routinely beat him up when he came back to the house. To put himself in the right mindset for the beatings, he developed a habit of visualizing the gruesome ordeal before it happened. Simply by mentally wiring himself before the beatings, he felt like he had more control over the situation. He had been administering part of the particular pain to himself, far from his father doing the same.

Many people suffering from social anxiety develop a similar mindset. By harming themselves mentally and pulling themselves down, they get to a point where they can't feel any worse. Most of the time, they have this belief this will prevent other people in social interactions from pulling them deeper into their anxiety misery. In their minds, they think this is the ideal way of being in control even though it causes pain and can stunt their social lives.

A majority of people are born with a temperament that is behaviorally inhibited. Just like the behaviorally inhibited temperament, so lies the problem of insecure attachment techniques in young ones. Two types of insecure attachment styles exist:

- *Anxious-equivocal insecure attachment.* This refers to being anxious of explorations and interactions with strangers even when the primary caregiver, which is usually the mother, is present.

- *Anxious-avoidant insecure attachment.* This is about not exploring much regardless of whether the caregiver is there, showing indifference and little emotional range toward other people.

A kid behaviorally learns to pull away from unfamiliar or nerve-racking scenarios and individuals, according to psychiatrist George Hadeed. The extinction from the fear simply by virtue of avoidance reinforces avoidant behavior later on in life and is seen as a protective reaction. Keep in mind that research reveals that temperament and attachment are usually both environmental and hereditary.

Genes as a Factor within Causing Social Anxiety

Researchers have not unearthed the gene that causes social panic. Nonetheless, there is a good aspect of heritability. When your parents have interpersonal anxiety, you happen to be most likely to have it. This is particularly true regardless of the associated environment.

Neurological Factors within Having Social Panic

People with social panic or social anxiety condition generally have hyperactivity in components of their brains plus imbalances of certain neurotransmitters. Here are some illustrations:

- hyperactivity in the amygdala as well as other limbic regions associated with the brain that procedure anxiety

- elevations in automatic emotional processing

- too much activity within the right prefrontal cortex, another section that influences social behavior

Technological Issues That Influence Social Anxiety Disorder

We live at a time when we don't need to spend much time interacting in person. Phone texting, social media, and a massive ton of apps enable people to stay in touch without meeting physically. There is a rise in the number of shows, TV games, and online content that people can consume rather than interacting with each other. According to Tom Kersting, a therapist and author of *Disconnected: How to Reconnect Our Digitally Distracted Kids*, in his research and experiences as a psychotherapist who counsels countless people, he believes that the shared environmental factor is that individuals are spending a lot of their morning sessions watching rather than talking to each other.

There is clinical evidence for a link between online communications and social anxiety. The younger people use online communication and texting in place of in-person interaction, the more likely they are to fear negative assessment and have social panic, based on a study that was carried out by the Islamic Azad University. A similar study done at the University of California demonstrated that while adolescents are most of the time confident with texting and online conversations, they are always anxious when it comes to face-to-face social interactions.

Physical Triggers That Cause Social Anxiety Symptoms

When people suffer from social anxiety or social anxiety disorder, certain physical events and triggers exist, and they spur anxious thoughts or physiological symptoms, including shortness of breath. Below are some examples of proven events and motivators:

- leaving home

- interactions with others, more so new people or guys in an unfamiliar environment, such as a party

- large crowds

- interactions where people may want to assess you, including interviews for work, public speaking, dating, etc.

- moving

- receiving a judgmental or disapproving stare

from a person

Comparing the origin of Social Anxiety and Social Anxiety Disorder

The starting points of these two phenomena are very much identical. The divergence however is that social anxiety disorder is worse, so the root causes are usually more severe or multilayered. Think of someone who grew up in a mentally healthy environment and has a secure temperament. He inherited some social anxiety from the mother, but he didn't have any traumatic encounters that exacerbated it. A person such as this is highly unlikely to develop a social anxiety disorder.

Now think about someone else who had an insecure attachment as a child and suffered abuse and bullying during his teenage years. In addition, the parents had social anxiety and raised him in a manner that nurtures socially anxious behavior. He is much more likely to have a social anxiety disorder, not just social anxiety. Social anxiety disorder gives rise to a lot of distress and can hinder people from leading a normal life. On the other hand, social anxiety is simpler to manage. Everyone encounters at least a little bit of social anxiety as they meet new people and make changes in their lives.

What Causes Social Anxiety in Adults as Compared to Children?

The causes of social anxiety in grown-ups and young ones are similar. Earlier happenings and surroundings are more likely to be elements in grown-ups flourishing social anxiety. Why is this so? The reason is due to the fact that they have had more time of going through trauma and socially anxious surroundings. When it comes to children, genetics and temperament can be more considerable factors.

Figuring Out That the Reasons Is the First Step to Finding the Best Treatment

Understanding the causes of interpersonal anxiety or social panic attacks can help you or someone you care about find a treatment that can lessen stress and symptoms. When the causes seem to be purely neurological, for instance, psychiatry might be the best approach. However, if the issues seem to be stemming from experiences, conditions, beliefs or behaviors, using talking as a remedy is the best long-term solution.

Symptoms of Social Anxiety

Dealing with unfamiliar situations and unfamiliar people can be difficult for anyone, but for someone struggling with social anxiety, that difficulty can increase ten times over. Most of the time, others don't recognize you're in the midst of a struggle. You may have developed techniques for coping to conceal the mental and emotional symptoms you're experiencing when you're social anxiety kicks in. However, when your body opts to take charge and you start experiencing physical symptoms, social anxiety can become increasingly noticeable. Selected people within a mental health community who struggle with social anxiety showed surprising physical symptoms they experience because of their social anxiety. It is evident that by talking about these physical symptoms, we can become more aware of our bodily responses, and we can become better at comforting ourselves and others in the midst of struggle.

Chapter Two:

Overcoming Social Anxiety

Therapy for Social Anxiety Disorder

The good thing is that cognitive-behavioral treatment for social anxiety has already been markedly successful. Research and clinical evidence alike show that cognitive-behavioral therapy that ought to be comprehensive produces lasting changes in the lives of people. Social anxiety disorder can be defeated even though it will take both consistency and persistence. Everyone can make progress against interpersonal anxiety using the appropriate type of cognitive-behavioral treatment. At several treatment centers, cognitive-behavioral treatment is applied for social panic and anxiety attacks. It is referred to as comprehensive cognitive-behavioral therapy to differentiate it from the entire proposition that apprehension notions are simplistic and can be taken care of by using only a few techniques.

A successful solution program for social panic and anxiety attacks must address all the intellectual methods, strategies, and principles that will allow individuals' brains to change literally. The brain is always under a repeated cycle of learning, and illogical thinking and values can change, hence this cognitive process. An excellent solution program will offer the required and specific strategies as well as reveal to the people how and why they have to practice, focus on, and begin to acknowledge rational thoughts, values, feelings, and perceptions.

Finding Help for Social Anxiety Disorder

Social anxiety, together with other anxiety disorders, can be successfully cured. While seeking support for this problem, you should also visit a specialist. Consult a person who:

- knows this problem well

- knows how to treat it from experience

Become an informed customer and ask questions. For example, does the counselor understand that you feel very self-conscious and that others are watching and forming a negative opinion about you? Or maybe they simplify what you're saying and just say, "No, no, you're fine . . . You're just exaggerating." It is a fact that people who have experienced interpersonal anxiety do realize that our minds are many times irrational and we exaggerate, but it still seems like others are watching and judging us. Our feeling of self-consciousness is quite real. If your psychologist or mental health-care worker does not understand this, you know more than they do about social anxiety. Under such a situation, it is very doubtful they will be in a position to help you. Also, keep in mind that the professional should always welcome your questions. If someone seems unfriendly or too scientific, steer clear of their advice and services.

People like me, and you, my reader, if you have experienced, or are going through social anxiety, we should be supported, encouraged, and stay in a relatively stress-free surrounding while under treatment so that our brain can absorb all the changes that are taking place without being damaged by external factors. If our environment is peaceful when undergoing treatment for social anxiety, it is easier to learn new habits that will completely change our thoughts, values, feelings, and our lives.

Did your therapist say something like "Face your fears, and they will disappear"? I am sorry to say this but this therapist has no idea what social anxiety is or what he or she is dealing with. As people who have experienced social panic, have constantly faced our fears ever since delivery. We have had to and also feel more fearful now than we did during the past. In this case, seek another counselor. It is imperative that you find a psychologist who understands social anxiety disorder adequately. If they don't even really know what it is, how can they really know what to do to help you overcome it?

Getting over social panic attacks is not a fairly easy job, nor is it a difficult one. A majority of people have already done it. While you're in the center of the social anxiety symptoms, it feels hopeless, and it seems that you'll never get any better. Yet this can be ceased, quenched, and killed in a relatively short timeframe. This can be done by finding a cognitive-behavioral therapist who knows and focuses on the treatment of social anxiety.

The Most Crucial Elements in Overcoming Interpersonal Anxiety

- an understanding and awareness of the problem

- a dedication to carry through with cognitive-behavioral treatment even when it is repetitious and seems difficult

- exercise and practice so that these cognitive methods become habitual and automated

- participation in a social anxiety treatment team in which you can slowly and steadily work on the issues that cause you anxiety in the real world

A person who feels stressed while reading in public areas utilizes specific strategies to meet his goal, whereas the one who wants to learn how to make introductions and take part in little conversations during social interactions gradually works toward his goals. We can use role plays, acting, question-and-answer periods, mock job selection interviews, and deliberately doing foolish things included in a reliable behavior treatment group for individuals with social anxiety.

Groups

Social anxiety behavior treatment groups must not pressure, push, or cajole people to do things. Simply no negative tactic should be employed because the person must choose to take part at his or her own speed. If someone wants to sit there in a team and not say a word, that's okay. Nobody should be coerced to do anything. You may think that people never make any improvements when they choose to do nothing in a group session. This has never happened. People in a group understand their issues and, under their own accord, choose to work on their specific anxieties. This approach is much more useful than being forced to do something.

Therapy groups for interpersonal anxiety should always be encouraging and positive. If the right atmosphere is placed, people can make and go on making progress up their ladder of social anxieties. It is impossible to prevent a motivated person who will not give up. The role of the therapist is to learn specifically what to do and how quickly to do it. This particularly seems simple even though it isn't. You must use the right material, and you need to move at the right pace for your own anxieties. You are more in control of this method than you think.

These days, cognitive-behavioral treatment can be used to deal with both kinds of social stress. With cognitive-behavioral therapy, we do not dwell on previous situations and continuously bring it up since it has no benefit. Alternatively, our focus should be on current troubles and signs and utilize several small techniques to eliminate anxiety thinking, feelings, beliefs, and belief systems. You might start having symptoms and getting anxious immediately before a celebration, or you might even spend weeks worrying about it. Afterward, you can spend a lot of time and mental energy worrying about how precisely you acted.

No one single thing causes interpersonal anxiety disorder. Genetics is likely to have something to do with it. If you have a family member who had social phobia, you are more likely to have it too. Interpersonal panic attacks usually come on at around thirteen years of age. It can be connected to a background of abuse, bullying, or teasing. Shy kids are also more likely to become socially anxious when they grow up, similar to children with overbearing or controlling parents. When you develop a health condition that draws attention to your appearance or voice, you could also be triggered to suffer from social anxiety.

Lots of people with social anxiety also exhibit other mental health issues, such as depression, generalized panic attacks, or body dysmorphic disorder.

When to Get Help for Social Panic

It's wise to see your specialist if you feel you have social anxiety, especially when it's having a major impact on your life. This is a common problem, and some treatments can be beneficial. It can be difficult to ask for help, but your specialist will be aware that many people have trouble with social anxiety and will attempt to put you at ease. Your specialist will ask you about your feelings, behaviors, and symptoms to determine the magnitude of your anxiety in social situations.

If they think you could have social panic, you'll be referred to a mental-health specialist to have a full assessment and weigh the treatment options. Moreover, you can also recommend yourself directly for mental therapies without seeing your doctor.

How You Can Overcome Social Stress

Social anxiety disorder can be very difficult to cope with even though there are some steps and actions that you can take the initiative to try. Furthermore, there is also a wide variety of medical options, treatments, and support groups that are quite beneficial.

Things You Can Try

Self-help may most probably not remedy your social anxiety, but it may reduce it, and you might find it an important first step before trying other treatments. The following tips may help:

- Try to understand more about your anxiety. What goes through your mind? How do you behave in some social situations? Knowing these things will help you get a clearer idea of the problems you want to tackle.

- Replace your unrealistic beliefs with increased rational ones. For instance, if you feel a social situation went badly, think if there are any facts to support this or if you are just assuming the worst.

- Avoid thinking too much about how exactly other people see you. Pay attention to other people. Remember that your stress symptoms aren't as obvious as you might think.

- Get involved in activities that you'd normally avoid. This is often tough at first. So start with small goals and work at more terrifying activities gradually.

Remedies for Social Panic

The primary options are as follows:

1. *Cognitive behavioral remedy (CBT) with a therapist.* This remedy is helpful in helping you identify negative thought patterns and behaviors and alter them.

2. *Self-help.* This requires you to work through a CBT-based workbook or online course with regular support from a therapist.

3. *Antidepressant medication.* This is usually a type of medicine called a picky serotonin reuptake inhibitor, or SSRI. The commonly known options are escitalopram or sertraline.

CBT is thought to be the best option for treatment even though other modes of treatment are effective in case it won't work or if you don't want to try it. Some individuals need to try a combination of treatments.

How Is Social Anxiety Disorder Treated?

First of all, visit your general physician or health-care specialist about how you feel. Your practitioner will carry out a test and inquire about your health history so as to ensure that an unrelated physical problem is not leading to your symptoms. Your family doctor may refer you to a mental health doctor—for example, a psychiatrist, psychologist, clinical social worker, or counselor. The initial action to adequate treatment is to have a diagnosis made, normally by a mental health doctor.

Social anxiety disorder is usually treated with psychotherapy, which is at times referred to as "talk" therapy, medication or both. Talk to your doctor or health-care provider about the best treatment for you.

Psychotherapy

A type of psychiatric therapy called cognitive behavioral remedy (CBT) is very useful for treating social panic disorder. CBT shows you different ways of thinking, acting, and reacting to situations that help you feel less anxious and afraid. Additionally, it may help you learn and practice social skills. CBT delivered in a group setting can be quite helpful.

Support Groups

Several people with social panic also find support groupings helpful. In a team of people who all have a social anxiety disorder, you can receive unbiased, sincere feedback about how others in the group feel about you. This way, you can learn that your thoughts about various views and rejection are not true or are distorted. You can also find out other people with social anxiety disorder overcome their fear of social interactions.

Medication

These are the three types of medications that are used in treating social stress disorder:

- anti-anxiety medications

- antidepressants

- beta-blockers

Anti-anxiety medications are powerful and start working immediately to reduce anxious feelings. However, such medicine is usually not prescribed for long periods. People's bodies can really get used to the medication if they are taken over a lengthy period. Consequently, their bodies may require higher doses so as to get the same effect. To avoid these problems, doctors usually prescribe anti-anxiety medications for short periods, a practice that is usually helpful for older patients.

Antidepressants are usually used to treat depression, but they can also help for the symptoms of social anxiety disorder. As opposed to anti-anxiety medications, they may take several weeks to begin working. Antidepressants may also have side effects, such as headaches, nausea, or difficulty in sleeping. Most of the time, these side effects are not severe for most people, particularly if the dose starts off low and is gradually increased over time. Consult your specialist about any undesirable drug effects that you may experience.

Beta-blockers are medications that can help prevent some of the physical symptoms of anxiety within the body such as an increased heart rate, perspiration, and tremors. Beta-blockers are most of the time the preferred medicine for the performance-anxiety type of social anxiety.

Work with your doctor to find the best medication, as well as the dose and period of treatment. Many people with social anxiety disorder realize the best results with a combination of medication and CBT or other psychotherapies. Don't give up on treatment too quickly. Both psychotherapy and medication can take a while to work. A healthy lifestyle can also help fight anxiety. Be sure you get enough sleep and exercise, eat a healthy diet, and turn to family and friends whom you trust for support.

Treatment for Social Anxiety Disorder

Several sorts of treatment are available for a social anxiety problem. Treatment results differ from person to person. A few individuals only need a single type of treatment while others may require more than one. Your health-care provider may refer you to a mental-health provider concerning your treatment. Sometimes, primary-care providers may recommend medication to treat symptoms. Treatment options for social anxiety disorder include the following:

Cognitive Behavioral Therapy

This treatment helps you learn how to control anxiety via relaxation and breathing and how to replace unfavorable thoughts with positive ones.

Exposure Therapy

This type of treatment helps you to progressively face

social situations rather than avoiding them.

Group Therapy

This treatment helps you learn social skills and techniques to socialize with individuals in social settings. Participating in group treatment with others who possess the same fears could make you feel less anxiety by yourself. It also offers an opportunity for you to exercise your brand-new skills through role-playing.

At-home treatments include the following:

1. *Staying away from coffee.* Coffee, chocolate, and soft drinks are stimulants and might increase anxiety.

2. *Having a lot of sleep.* Getting a minimum of eight hours of sleep every night is recommended. The absence of sleep can increase anxiety and worsen signs and symptoms of social phobia.

Your own health-care provider may recommend medications that treat stress and depression in case your situation doesn't improve through treatment and lifestyle changes. Medicines given the green light by the Food and Drug Administration (FDA) to treat social panic attacks consist of Paxil, Zoloft, and Effexor XR. Your doctor should start with the low doses of medicine and slowly increase your own prescription to avoid side effects.

Common side effects of these medications include the following:

- insomnia or sleeplessness

- weight gain

- stomach upsets

- reduced sexual desire

Talk with your health-care specialist about the pros and cons so that you can make up your mind about the kind of treatment that you fit in.

A point of view for Social Anxiety Disorder

According to the ADAA, roughly one third of people suffering from social anxiety never consult a health-care professional until they have suffered for a minimum of ten years. People suffering from a social anxiety disorder may depend on drugs and alcohol to cope with anxiety that is caused by social interaction. If left untreated, social phobia can lead to other high-risk behaviors, such as alcohol and drug abuse, loneliness, and thoughts of suicide. The future of social anxiety disorder looks bright with treatment. Therapies, changes in the way of living, and medicine can assist a good number of people to cope with their anxiety disorders and lead normal lives.

Social phobia doesn't have to control your life. Even though it may stretch over a long period, psychotherapy and/or medication can help a lot. Keep your own fears under control simply by doing the following:

- recognizing the triggers that will cause you nervousness

- practicing relaxation and breathing methods

- taking your own medication as directed

Interpersonal anxiety disorder symptoms can change as time passes. However, they can explode if you are facing a lot of stressful situations or life demands. Even though avoiding situations that trigger your condition may offer you short-term relief, your anxiety is likely to go on for years if you don't get treatment.

When to See a Physician

Just like many other mental health conditions, social anxiety condition is also likely to arise from a complex interaction of natural and environmental factors. Some of the causes include the following:

- *Inherited qualities.* Anxiety disorders often run in families even though it isn't fully clear how much of this may be due to genes or how much as a result of learned behavior.

- *Brain construction.* A structure in the mind called the amygdala may play a role in controlling the worry reaction. People who have an overactive amygdala could possibly have a heightened fear response and triggering increased anxiety in interpersonal situations.

- *Environment.* Social panic disorder may be a learned behavior. A lot of people may develop the condition after an upsetting or uncomfortable social situation.

Danger Factors

Several factors can encourage the risk of developing social anxiety disorder, including the following:

- *Family history.* You have higher chances of developing social anxiety disorder in case your biological parents or siblings have the condition.

- *Negative experiences.* Kids who are teased, bullied,

rejected, ridiculed, or humiliated may be more vulnerable to social anxiety disorder. Additionally, other undesired events in life, such as conflicts within the family, trauma, or abuse, may be linked to social anxiety disorder.

- *Temperament.* Kids who are withdrawn when facing new situations or people may be highly vulnerable.

- *New social or work demands.* Symptoms of social anxiety disorder basically kick in during the teenage years even though making contact with new people, offering a public talk, or giving a crucial work presentation may trigger signs.

Complications

If left untreated, social anxiety disorder can run your life. Anxiety disorders can get in the way of one's work, school, personal relationships, or other joys of life. Social anxiety disorder can cause the following:

- low self-esteem

- trouble being assertive

- negative self-talk

- hypersensitivity to criticism

- poor social skills

- solitude and difficult social human relationships

- low academic and work attainment

- drug abuse, such as excessive alcohol intake

- suicide or committing suicide tries

Other anxiety problems and certain other psychological health disorders, particularly major depressive disorder and compound abuse problems, often occur together with social panic attacks.

Avoidance

There's no way to predict what can cause anyone to develop a panic disorder. You could take steps to reduce the impact of symptoms by doing the following:

- *Getting help earlier.* Anxiety, just like many other mental-health issues, can be harder to deal with if you procrastinate.

- *Keeping a record.* Keeping track of your individual life can help you, as well as your mental-health professional, identify what's triggering your stress and what appears to help you feel better.

- *Prioritizing issues in your life.* You can minimize the

effects of anxiety by rationally organizing your time and energy. Ensure that you spend time doing things you enjoy.

- *Avoiding unhealthy substance use.* Alcohol and drug use, caffeine, or even nicotine use can cause or worsen anxiety. In case you are addicted to any of these substances, quitting can make you anxious. When you can't quit on your own, consult your doctor or find a treatment program or support group to help you.

Social Anxiety Triggers

Individuals who suffer from social anxiety do not exude the signs during every social interaction. On the other hand, when they collaborate with people they are familiar with and are sure they can trust, such as partners, parents, siblings, children, grandparents, close friends, long-time employers, and favorite teachers, chances are they may fail to exhibit signs of social anxiety in any way. Additionally, in case they have to deliver a public speech about their areas of specialization, they do so with great belief in themselves. However, several other situations evoke great distress and anxiety even though they wouldn't appear threatening to a majority of people. Some of the commonly known and studied motivators for social anxiety patients are as follows:

- meeting new people

- internet dating

- interactions with authority statistics

- conversations with extroverts

- celebrations, especially when the social panic sufferer is attending alone

- large family gatherings where not everyone is acquainted

- unexpected attempts to start conversations by others in public places

- being teased or kidded (people with social panic disorder most of the time take teasing personally)

- being watched while performing an unfamiliar task

- being requested to speak before a course or a room full of co-workers

- speaking on the phone, especially with other people

A lot of people with social panic disorder have three or

four situations that cause overwhelmingly anxious reactions, and they'll go to great measures to avoid these exposures if they possibly can. Other social situations may produce more moderate panic symptoms, but even these are unpleasant and make life more difficult than it should be.

Getting Help for Social Panic Disorder

If undiagnosed and without treatment, social anxiety disorder is a devastating condition that can severely limit daily functioning. Even when interpersonal sufferers of anxiety realize they have a serious problem, it is still always difficult to request for help. Additionally, therapists are specialists and people with social anxiety disorder generally avoid interactions with specialists as much as they can. But the truth of the matter is that social anxiety is a condition that is highly responsive to treatment, and when patients do gather the courage to ask for help, they often achieve great outcomes.

Even though medications are most of the time options offered by doctors for those with interpersonal anxiety disorder, psychotherapy is the core of interpersonal anxiety treatment. Cognitive-behavioral treatments (CBT) in particular has been found to be effective against social anxiety's most disabling symptoms and is almost always suggested by mental health specialists who see social panic disorder patients. Most treatments for social anxiety require placing a patient on an outpatient basis. However, people who have struggled with social panic attacks for many years can gain great benefit from inpatient stays in a mental health treatment service where all the concentration is on recovery.

Within residential treatment programs, CBT and other essential services will be offered in a compassionate, patient-centered atmosphere. Peer interactions are usually included in residential interpersonal anxiety disorder recovery programs, giving social-anxiety patients a unique and important possibility to interact with others who face similar life challenges and be familiar with the hurdles of triumphing over them.

This condition is stressful to bear, however, with the use of specialists and medication, it's controllable. Interpersonal anxiety can be both frustrating and fascinating. When you experience it, a person might wonder, "What leads to my social anxiety? Why do I have to cope with this?" Even if you don't have it, you may be curious. Maybe someone you care for has it, or you're thinking about exploring the issues surrounding it. Whatever the reason may be, having knowledge of what social anxiety is, isn't a waste. Having adequate knowledge will enable you to empathize with the approximately fifteen million individuals who suffer from it. If you are suffering from this condition and it stresses you out, learning what leads to it is the very first step to treating this. There are seven wide types of causes for interpersonal anxiety:

- past encounters and environments as well as impacts associated with parenting style, trauma, and so on

- negative beliefs plus maladaptive behavior

- behaviorally inhibited temperament and insecure connection style

- genetics, where one is most likely to have social panic if relatives have it

- neurology, which is associated with overactivity in specific areas of the brain linked to anxiety

- the influence of technology where people are usually spending less time conferencing in person and meeting people face-to-face

- physical causes, such as being in situations and events that will make men and women feel socially anxious or trigger signs and symptoms of social anxiety disorder

Each factor influences several of the others. Bad environments and experiences associated with social interactions often result in men and women developing bad beliefs and maladaptive behaviors. These beliefs and behaviors may cause and nurture interpersonal anxiety. The cognitive results then change brain construction and functioning.

Genetics, character, and attachment styles make this condition pretty much likely to happen. As soon as men and women develop social panic, various triggers make them experience symptoms, including isolating themselves or panicking.

To explore these factors further, keep on reading!

Overcoming Social Anxiety

Earlier on, I talked about the nature and frequency of social anxiety. When you find yourself inhibited and anxious in a variety of social situations, such as speaking in front of an organization, meeting new people, using public lockers or restrooms or even eating in public, and you also fear that people will see your panic and that you can feel humiliated, then you may be suffering from social panic disorder. Many people with this issue will choose to avoid situations where they anticipate being anxious, or they might use alcohol or drugs to self-medicate before entering these situations. Interpersonal anxiety is associated with increased risk for alcoholic beverages abuse, depression, loneliness, reduced occupational advancement, and the increased likelihood of staying single.

Cognitive behavioral counselors make great advances for a drug-free approach to dealing with these problems. Right now, there is now considerable proof that CBT (cognitive behavior therapy) is an effective treatment for social anxiety. This particular remedy focuses on your behavior and what you are thinking. So let's delve deeper and find out how beneficial this therapy is at getting over social anxiety.

The particular behavioral problem for those with social anxiety is the tendency to avoid anxiety-provoking situations. When the socially anxious individual anticipates heading to a celebration, he or she becomes quite anxious. However, when he chooses not to go, the anxiety immediately subsides. This reduction of panic with the decision to avoid the party or to leave a party strengthens avoidance or escape. This simple reward for avoidance confirms the concern of negative social examination even when the individual really does not experience humiliation. For example, if I feel stressed thinking of approaching someone and then I decide to avoid talking with him or her, my panic immediately subsides. This immediate decrease in anxiety dictates that for me to feel less anxious, I should just avoid interacting with other people.

A key factor of CBT is to help the individual practice

approaching social situations and stay in them to learn that nothing really bad will probably happen and that their anxiety will subside. A person also learns that he can do it and the simple willingness to confront his fears is empowering. You start realizing that you are not the sort of person who can actually try and face their fears. The initial move in assisting people with this condition identifying the scenarios that they are avoiding. You can make a listing of the types of situations that you feel anxious in or avoid. For instance, one person realized that using a public toilet where he was worried that individuals watch him, interacting with strangers at a party, speaking during meetings, and speaking to a woman for the first time were some of his anxiety triggers. What are the situations that provoke your anxiety? What are you likely to avoid? Make a listing.

Setting Up a Hierarchy of Fear

For every situation, you can identify how the situation could be rated in terms of how much anxiety you would experience. You can rate each anticipated response on a scale of 0 to 10, depending on the level of anxiety that you might expect—0 would mean there is no anxiety while 10 would signify a panic attack. For instance, a young man with the fear of meeting people at a party experienced the following stages of fear, from the lowest to the highest. Thinking of going to the party rates at 3, going to the party is at 5, walking into the room ranked at 6, seeing people in the room is also number 6, deciding to begin a conversation rests at number 8, and talking with a stylish woman is at 9. It's important to write down your predictions to be able to find a way of discovering how anxious you really are as you go. At times, people realize that they are not as anxious as they anticipated they would be.

Test Your Predictions

We often forget the fact that we deal better than we thought we would. This is a great chance to test your particular forecasts. As earlier discussed, you can jot down how anxious you predict you will be in everything. What is the extent of the expected anxiety? How long will you remain that anxious? Specifically, what do you predict will happen? This is how you can test your catastrophic fortune-telling. For instance, a young man who was socially anxious predicted that he might have a level of anxiety at 9 for the whole length of speaking with a woman at a celebration. He predicted that his mind would go empty and that he would be so anxious that he would need to go. As it unfolded, he was full ofanxiety when he started the discussion, however, once he was immersed in the talk, his level of being anxious reduced to three. He never left, and he got the impression that the woman he was speaking with actually liked him. Therefore, be clear about what you are predicting so as to find out if you are anticipating more than what actually happens. Maintain a continuous record of your predictions.

Determine Your Protective Traits and Get Rid of Them

A majority of people who suffer from anxiety get involved in mythical conduct that they believe could get them to safety or less likely to humiliate themselves. These safety behaviors include self-medicating with alcoholic beverages or drugs, holding yourself very stiffly, avoiding attention contact, holding a cup tightly so that people will not see your hands trembling, wiping your hands so that men and women won't notice you are sweating, rehearsing verbatim what exactly you will say, and talking very fast. The problem with protective behaviors is that they are like the training tires on a bicycle, and they allow you to believe the only way you can get through these experiences is to use the training wheels.

Chapter Three:

The Power of Meditation and Relaxation to Ease Anxiety

The word *meditation* originates from the Latin word *meditatio* and means "to think, ponder, or contemplate." Meditation is a way of transforming the mind and body through techniques that enhance and develop concentration and positivity. It is a method of deep relaxation that rests the mind and, in turn, the body.

Simply put, meditation is peace of mind!

The aim of meditation is to achieve self-regulation of the mind by using the various meditation techniques for relaxation, mental clarity, and building positive internal energy. It is this end that helps to manage health problems, like anxiety, depression, and high blood pressure.

The body is nourished and healed through rest. You achieve deep rest and relaxation through meditation;

therefore, it is great for rejuvenating the body to leave you well and mentally serene. Research has shown that the degree of rest achieved when one is meditating is greater than that harnessed from sleep. The findings are incredible. Twenty minutes of deep meditation has been equated to seven hours of sleep!

The desired goal of mental clarity, positivity, and peace is reached through regular practice of meditative techniques. For maximum harvest of the benefits, be committed to this art. In the course of time, your body will get into a rhythm and in tune for inner peace.

Brief History

Meditation has a long and rich history. This mental and physical wellness art is dated as far back as some of the old civilizations and religions. Meditation is closely interlinked to religion in many of the places where it is traditionally practiced and may have its roots in religion.

Meditation techniques were employed for the attainment of a higher purpose in the pursuit of divine perfection and to bring one closer to the creator. Research has it that the earliest evidence of meditation is in Hindu scriptural texts. It is from these beginnings that other forms of meditation developed in Asia and the Orient. In the sixth and fifth century, meditation has been adopted by Taoists in China and Hindus, Jains, and Buddhists in India.

In Islam, Sufism, and Dhikr, meditation is practiced through word repetitions, chants, movements, and controlled breathing. In the West, Christian meditation picked up around the sixth century during Bible readings among Benedictine monks. Modern forms of meditation that most of us practice today appeared in India in the 1950s as secular forms of meditation techniques that are more geared toward reduction of stress, self-improvement, and relaxation. The modern forms of meditation do not focus on spirituality.

In fact, meditation was used by these religions as techniques for bringing practitioners closer to God, for the closer one was to God, the more peaceful they were and the more clarity of mind they attained. With this brief history and knowledge of meditation, let us look at the different types and techniques of meditation practiced around the world in the next section.

Types or Techniques of Meditation

There are many different types and techniques of meditation that we shall not be able to cover everything. Meditative techniques are in the hundreds but are all linked by the common thread of aiming at achieving inner peace for the practitioner.

First and foremost, all meditative practices engage in mind-control techniques as a way to achieve relaxation and peace. Second, there are postures and body movements that are found in all forms of meditation. These two traits are evident in all meditative practices pointing to a common goal for all of them.

Meditation helps to relieve our bodies and minds of the toxic effects of stress. It relaxes us and brings the peace of mind that we all yearn for. Before you pick up one form of meditation or another, it is important to do your research and learn as much as you can about them. Interrogate yourself. Find out and decide what your meditative goals are or would be to help you pick up the right technique for you.

In some cases, you will need to get a teacher or join a meditation school for the right advice, coaching, and mentorship in taking up meditation. There are types of meditative practices that cannot be performed by beginners, people with certain conditions or illnesses, or older people for example. Seeking the right information will guide you to the right technique. It is also important to remember to take on a meditative practice that will fit your lifestyle. Meditation requires consistency, regularity, discipline, and high commitment for one to realize the desired fruits. With the many types of meditation in existence, we can generally categorize meditation as follows:

Concentrative Meditation

In concentrative meditation, the mind is directed to a particular object, chant/mantra, sound, or sensation. The practitioner will focus their mind and energy on a focal point of their choosing that best works for them in an effort to clear and calm their minds and bodies. These types of meditations are good for beginners.

Mindfulness Meditation

This type of meditation does not rely on focusing the mind on an object but relies on feelings, sensations, emotions and thought patterns to achieve a meditative state. These are more advanced types of meditation that are not for everyone, especially beginners.

Effortless Transcending

This type of meditation is referred to as "effortless" because there is no mental effort or concentration required. Some call this technique of meditation "pure being" or "transcendental" because it is about emptiness, introversion, and calmness. The aim here is to help the practitioner recognize their true essence or the true nature of the self by eliminating all thought.

With consistent practice, the mind becomes an open space that allows for relaxation. It has been compared to massaging the brain. The transcendental process will help the practitioner silence their mind and become aware of a deep state of consciousness. People who practice this specific type may experience a state of emptiness or nothingness and find that it feels great.

Below are some types of meditation:

1. Buddhist Meditation

Zen Meditation (Zazen). Zazen is Japanese meaning "seated Zen" or "seated meditation," referring to the form of Zen meditation practiced while sitting. Zazen originates from Chinese Zen Buddhism. It is done while seated on the floor, usually on a mat, with crossed legs. This was traditionally done in the lotus or half-lotus position.

For the mind, Zazen employs two techniques:

- Focus on breathing. The practitioner will pay attention to the inhalation and exhalation while silently counting down with every breath and back.

- Shikantanza. Here, there is no specific object of meditation. One remains in the moment being aware of what goes through their mind and what passes around.

Vipassana Meditation. Vipassana means clear seeing or insight and is a Buddhist type of meditation. It is ideal for mental discovery and awareness. It starts with mindfulness of breath to stabilize and focus the mind (focused-mind meditation). Then it moves to developing clarity of awareness of bodily sensations and mental phenomena. Sit on the floor, legs crossed, with a straight back.

Mindfulness Meditation. Mindfulness meditation combines practices from various Buddhist meditation practices. It is widely employed in hospitals and other health benefits as a form of treatment. Here, the practitioner will focus on the moment while not losing awareness of thoughts and emotions experienced.

Religious/Spiritual Meditation. These are meditative practices that are practiced among the different religions. Remember that spirituality is one avenue for achieving peace of mind and relaxation. Here, meditation and prayer are combined to achieve spiritual development by reflection of God's Word. Meditation is a communion with the self with the aim of spiritual development or divinity.

Meditation in religion is practiced for peace of mind by steadying and focusing it to give the practitioner the ability for divine insight. A practitioner of Christian meditation said that God is sought through the study of scripture, but through meditation, he is found. There are forms of meditative practices in almost all religions, which prove the close link between spirituality and meditation.

Sufism meditative practices are some of the most elaborate of religious meditation. Practitioners get into a rhythm of chanting and movement that eventually transports participants into a spiritual realm. In Christianity, there are examples with the Catholics and Orthodox sects that have mantras or repetitive prayers.

Metta Meditation. It is also referred to as loving-kindness meditation and has its root in Tibet. This meditative form enhances empathy and compassion to make one more loving to self and others. The practitioner will sit and close their eyes, then generate feelings of kindness and compassion in their mind toward themselves then progress to others. Just like the name suggests, this type of meditation aims at creating harmony with one's surrounding. Treat all things with kindness, and the rewards are happiness and compassion for you. You emit happiness, and the world bounces it back to you.

2. Hindu Meditations

Vedic and Yogic forms of meditation are Hindu forms and are classified as follows:

Mantra Meditation. Mantra involves the repetition of a word or phrase to focus one's mind.

Transcendental   Meditation.   Transcendental techniques aim at opening the mind.

Yoga Meditation. *Yoga* means "union," and there are many types. Yoga combines mind relaxing and focusing practices with stretching movements and postures. Of all the meditative practices, yoga is the most popular of the secular forms of meditation and has the most following for nonreligious or spiritual meditation. You will find that most people who meditate are practicing one form of yoga or another.

How then do we use these techniques for self-improvement and relaxation? Let us first know the benefits of meditation.

Benefits of Meditation

There are several benefits apart from the ones we have discussed in the preceding sections. It is no wonder then that meditation is being promoted as an alternative to clinical treatment for cure and management of several health conditions and for general well-being. Meditation leads the body to undergo a change. Cells in the body are injected with more energy resulting in peace, happiness, and motivation as the energy levels in the body are boosted.

Below are the benefits of meditative practices:

1. Meditation reverses or reduces the production of stress hormones (adrenaline) by creating calmness and eradicating anxiety to prevent chronic stress. With controlled or regulated stress hormones, the body is more relaxed.

2. It is good for managing blood pressure and other heart diseases or conditions since the heart rate and breathing are slowed down. When we are not stressed, worried, or anxious, the heart rate is slow; therefore, the blood pressure is also low. Meditation can help greatly with conditions like high blood pressure since it works to create calmness and relaxation.

3. Boosts the immune system and slows aging as a result of less production of adrenaline by the body. The immune system is boosted since one ends up being healthier as a result of the suppression of destructive stress chemicals.

4. Meditation brings clarity of the mind, and creativity is enhanced. With a relaxed mind, one is sure to be more creative and productive.

5. Meditative techniques advocate for a pure life, and in fact, the aim of meditation is to attain purity akin to the higher being, so practitioners find themselves quitting poisonous habits, like smoking, drug abuse, and alcohol consumption.

6. Brain functioning is greatly improved through the

boosting of psychological creativity, a better memory, and a settled, relaxed mind.

7. Meditation makes you happier since your mind and body feel better. A relaxed person has no worries and will be a happier person.

8. You will sleep better since you are relaxed, enabling you to have more rest and better rest to face the day and tasks that you are faced with.

9. Meditation reduces how fast we age through mental and physical exercise. People who meditate have a slower aging process. Stress hormones hasten aging while meditation is known to halt or significantly reduce their production.

10. Meditation reduces or eliminates stress. A meditation practitioner is a calm and happy individual who is essentially immune to the effects of stress.

11. A relaxed and happier person has the benefit of a better functioning body. Immunity is boosted, and diseases are kept at bay.

12. When one embraces meditation with all its tenets and understands it, they hold life to a greater value since they learn the true meaning and purpose of living.

13. Meditative exercises improve metabolism and help

regulate weight by fighting obesity.

14. Meditation helps you feel more connected and in tune with yourself.

15. Meditation brings emotional balance and harmony.

16. Personal transformation is inevitable with meditation. You end up being a new person.

It is recommended that you meditate at least once a day for optimal results. Dawn meditation is highly recommended usually between 3:00 a.m. and 6:00 a.m. Dawn meditation is considered more beneficial as you tend to be more alert and well rested after your sleep. The environment is also quiet and ideal for meditation. In the next part, we shall learn how to use meditation to reduce stress in your life.

How to Reduce Stress by Meditating

So what is stress? Stress is basically the body's way of responding to pressure that may be exerted on it physically or psychologically. Stress is caused when the body releases stress chemicals, usually adrenaline, into the blood in an effort to combat whatever pressure it is confronted with. Stress can be classified as follows:

• Survival stress. This is stress that we face when

we are confronted by dangerous situations where you feel that physical harm is imminent. It is here where we have fight-and-flight response to fight stress.

- Internal stress. This is stress caused by worries over things that are out of your control. Simply put, internal stress is self-imposed stress that can be avoided by not giving yourself so much pressure over things that are beyond you.

- Environmental stress. This is stress caused by factors in your surrounding, like noise. Stay away from environmental stress triggers, and you will have a happy life.

- Tiredness. This type of stress is caused by fatigue, which usually accumulates over a long period due to such things as overworking.

Stress is an inescapable part of life, and sooner or later, we experience it. What we need to do is learn how to manage it so that it does not overwhelm us and take over our lives. Stress is not an entirely bad thing as it can enhance our alertness and concentration. However, in excess, it is very unhealthy.

Symptoms of stress

How do you know if you are stressed? The following

are some signs that will let you know if you are stressed.

Cognitive symptoms:

- problems remembering things

- low concentration

- high anxiety

- constant worry

Emotional symptoms:

- being moody

- highly irritable and angry

- loneliness and reclusion

- sadness

Physical symptoms:

- low libido

- aches and pain

- high heart rate

- dizziness

Behavioral symptoms:

- eating disorders (bingeing or self-starving)

- lack of sleep

- substance abuse

- nervousness

Causes of Stress

External causes:

- major life changes (divorce, chronic illness, the death of a loved one)

- work burden

- financial problems

- trauma

Internal causes:

- constant worry

- negativity and pessimism

- fear and anxiety

- unrealistic expectations

Stress can cause serious health and social problems if it is not dealt with immediately and well. Here are some of the side effects of stress:

- mental disorders, like depression and anxiety

- cardiovascular problems (high blood pressure, heart disease, stroke, etc.)

- weight problems, such as obesity

- problems with menstrual cycles

- skin and hair problems (acne, hair loss, etc.)

- sexual dysfunction

- gastrointestinal problems, like ulcers

Meditation and Stress Management

Meditation has been proven as a stress reliever and is being embraced by many for relaxation. Stress relief needs both mental and physical relaxation, and meditation provides that. To understand why meditation is so helpful in reducing stress, we should know what it takes to relax:

Deep breathing. Deep breathing is a quick and sure way of deflating stress from your system. This is a simple technique with far-reaching positive consequences in keeping stress in check.

Balancing the nervous system. For the body to function optimally, the nervous system must be at equilibrium. You must be at peace mentally. Stress destabilizes this balance, and the only way to stead your system is by relaxation. A state of profound serenity of the nervous system is the counter to stress.

Yoga

Yoga is a series of steady movement and stationary poses combined with deep breathing. Yoga reduces stress and improves flexibility, strength, balance, and stamina if practiced regularly. Almost all types of yoga are beneficial for stress and anxiety relief as they combine steady movement, deep breathing, and stretching. You may try the following types:

Satyananda. This is a traditional form of yoga that uses meditation, gentle poses, and deep relaxation and is ideal for those who want to start practicing for stress and anxiety relief.

Hatha Yoga. This is also a gentle form that is ideal for you to ease your way into practicing.

Power Yoga. Power yoga is more advanced and is for those who are already familiar with the basics. It is more intense, and the focus is fitness. This is ideal for those seeking relaxation and stimulation.

Tai Chi

Tai Chi is a mellow form of meditation suited for everyone. It is especially good for the elderly recovering from injuries and illnesses common with those of advanced age. It is a series of slow body movements, emphasizing concentration, circulation of energy through the body, and relaxation while focusing on breathing.

For you to effectively deal with stress and anxiety through meditation, it is important to be consistent in practicing whichever type of meditation you settle for. Make it part of your life. Practice it regularly until it becomes second nature. Here are what you need to do for a successful stress-relieving meditation experience:

- Get a quiet, serene place for your meditation exercise; this can be anywhere as long as it has no interference. It can be in your backyard, living room, in a park, etc.

- Assume a comfortable posture, whether seated, standing, or lying down. Start tuning your mind to the here and now. Focus and concentrate.

- In the posture with eyes closed, take a slow deep breath and relax your body as you do this. Get into an inhaling and exhaling rhythm.

- Clear your mind of distracting thoughts and

concentrate on your meditation. Pay attention to your breathing, and concentrate on that only as you relax.

- Channel your mind to happy thoughts of a happy place you have been, or just concentrate on the present while listening to your breathing. Push out unwanted thoughts that may come your way.

- Keep your eyes closed, take deep breaths, and imagine your body relaxing. Keep doing this until you are completely relaxed.

Imagine a life of reduced anxiety and stress. Isn't that what we all want? By following the advice and tips discussed above, you will be able to effectively kick out stress from your life and remain a happy and relaxed individual. Whenever stress is left to get out of control, depression sets in. Depression is a condition that is directly linked to the mismanagement of stress. Depression is the extreme form of stress. Let us understand what depression is and how meditation can help in its relief.

Fighting Depression through Meditation

In this section, we shall look at how meditation can be adopted in management and cure of depression and why it is gaining acceptance as an alternative to clinical medicine in the treatment and management of this condition. Depression is a disorder of a person's mood or emotions, causing sadness and loss of interest.

When one if faced with extreme emotions or feelings of hopelessness, anxiety, sadness, despair, or low self-esteem, they can be considered depressed. This type of depression is situational as it is triggered by circumstances that the person is dealing with. Clinically, depression is caused by chemical imbalance in the brain, causing bipolar disorder and manic depression, which are generally referred to as organic depression. Stress hormones (cortisol and epinephrine) found in adrenaline has been proven responsible for organic depression.

Depression is usually exhibited or accompanied by the following symptoms:

- loss of interest in hobbies and usual activities

- reclusiveness

- feelings of hopelessness and worthlessness

- difficulty or lack of sleep

- restlessness and fatigue

- lower concentration

- suicidal thoughts

Once in a while, we all face some form of mild depression. Unfortunately, some of us experience extreme forms of this condition that can overwhelm them leading to significant mental deterioration, social self-exclusion, and even suicides.

Causes of Depression

Depression is caused by a number of factors or, in some instances, a combination of these factors. They are as follows:

- encounters with stressful events (events such as the death of a loved one or the breakdown of a relationship)

- chronic and long illness

- some personality traits are more vulnerable to depression (e.g., low self-esteem)

- family history (those from families where some have suffered depression before are highly likely to be affected)

- giving birth (some women get postnatal depression because of physical and emotional changes)

- loneliness and drug abuse

- chemical changes in the brain (clinical depression)

- physical and emotional abuse

- some medicines

- conflicts

The good news is that depression can significantly be managed and even treated through meditation as we shall learn herein.

How Does Meditation Help Deal with Depression?

When we think about how we can fight depression by meditative means, we need to understand both and know how they correlate. We have seen in both situational and organic definitions that depression is a mental disorder caused by triggers that will destabilize the mental balance. Conversely, we have seen that meditation has been proven and is being used by many to reinstate this elusive balance.

In fact, all types of meditation have their foundations in the pursuit of a balanced mind where depression is not welcome. The many meditative techniques for mental focus and exercise are the reason meditation works to curb problems with depression. Meditation will teach you the techniques necessary for mental clarity and serenity with regular practice and adoption into your life. You will learn positive mental focusing for a healthy and calm mind.

When the mind is so balanced, one becomes more positive, happy, and optimistic. These attributes manifested as a result of meditative practice are what will keep you from getting depressed. The biggest secret of meditation is the ability to change one's thought process if embraced and practiced over time. Changing the way we think to be able to negate and effectively deal with negative situations and thought is the fundamental lesson of meditation. We need to take control of our minds to deal with our environment.

Bipolar and manic depressants can also gain a lot in management and even get cured of their condition through meditation. Using prescription medicine, the medical world is recommending and using meditation for the treatment of these conditions, and it is working! Meditation is making these patients calmer by focusing their thoughts and mental energies positively. It trains them how to control their mental emotions in circumstances that may exacerbate or trigger problems.

The ability to fight depression goes to the core of the goals of meditation, which is to elevate the mind to a level of self-regulation. Self-regulation leads to self-control, which spawns mental positivity, and a positive, happy mind cannot be depressed. Therefore, the mental and physical exercises found in meditation are essential for defeating depression. A healthy mind, together with a fit strong body, is a balance that is not easily tipped by mental emotions.

Research has shown that meditation works to eliminate or control depression by boosting one's social behavior and emotional well-being, which can work very well for cases of situational depression. Additionally, meditation has been proven to lower the levels of stress hormones released by the body that are responsible for depression. Adrenaline causes panic, which in turn causes depression if not checked or well managed. Meditative practices serve to calm a person down, thus regulating the production of these hormones.

Meditation will also train and help you detach yourself from emotional stress and still deal effectively with difficult situations to avoid the load of depression. In the next part, let us learn how to achieve the ultimate state of relaxation through meditation.

Using Meditation to Achieve Relaxation

Relaxation is a state of mental and physical calmness and serenity where one is free from tension and anxiety. Meditation practices reduce muscle tension, lower blood pressure, calm the mind, and eliminate stress in general. A response christened "relaxation response" is elicited when one is relaxed. It is the opposite of the stress response that is experienced when one is under pressure. Meditation is one sure way of generating the relaxation response.

Regular meditation will regularly generate the relaxation response, giving you more control of your body for a stress-free life. The following are the most used relaxation techniques:

Progressive muscle relaxation. This technique is used for relaxing deep muscle tension. Tension in the muscles increases anxiety, and this technique will reduce muscle tension and lower the heart rate and blood pressure. It can be practiced while lying on your back or seated. You tense each muscle group for a few seconds and relax. This is repeated until the whole body relaxes.

Deep breathing. Deep breathing emphasizes breathing control and focusing on your breathing to achieve a relaxed state. Take deep breaths from the stomach breathing in enough air into your lungs. Deep breaths mean more oxygen into your system. More oxygen means less tension and anxiety. Deep breathing is simple, but it is a powerful relaxation technique that is easily learned by all and can be done almost anywhere. It offers a quick fix for managing stress levels.

Remember that deep breathing is the basis of other relaxation techniques, and it can be applied together with other relaxation tools like aromatherapy and music. You can use the following routine for your deep breathing meditative technique:

- Sit with your back straight. Place a hand on your chest and the other hand on your stomach. The hands should guide you through the breathing routine.

- Breathe in using your nose. The hand placed on your tummy will be pushed up while the other on your chest will move very little.

- Breathe out from your mouth, releasing the most air you can manage while constricting your stomach muscles. The hand placed on your stomach will move inward as you breathe out while the will hardly move.

- Continue breathing in using your nose and exhaling through your mouth. Breathe in sufficient air so that your lower tummy rises and drops.

- Count down slowly as you breathe out.

- If breathing from your abdomen is a problem while you are seated, lie on a flat surface. The floor is ideal.

- Place a light visible object on your tummy to act as a guide and then breathe so that the object rises as you breathe in and falls as you breathe out.

Tense/Relax method. This technique is similar to progressive relaxation where you tense and relax muscles for relaxation.

Autogenic method. Autogenic method is also about muscle control to make one calmer and relaxed.

Guided imagery or visualization method. This can be used in conjunction with progressive relaxation or by itself. After you have relaxed your muscles, you can get into the visualization method, and use mental imagery to relax your mind. Visualization method is a variation on traditional forms of meditation techniques that require that you use all senses—vision, taste, feel/touch, hearing, and smell. Visualization method entails the creation of an image in your mind that leaves you feeling at peace and free to release all tension and anxiety.

Self-hypnosis. Self-hypnosis is a form of guided meditation that involves listening to a recording to access a deep state of relaxation. Once you reach a state of deep relaxation as possible, you are more open to suggestions, giving the hypnotherapist the opportunity to target and improve a particular aspect of thought.

Standard meditation. There are many types of standard guided meditations, many having different aims and purposes. Guided meditations are not the same, so you ought to know which one you are using and for what purpose it is.

Body scan. This is a type of guided meditation where a recording will instruct the practitioner to focus on a specific part of the body and identify any tension. Body scanning entails heightened awareness of any stressor pain in certain parts of the body. A body scan can be performed while seated or lying down comfortably. A full body scan can take a long time (up to one hour), but shorter versions are still highly effective.

Brainwave meditation. This type of meditation targets brainwaves for stress relief and relaxation. Brainwave meditations start out with a guiding voice, which is usually just relaxing music and sounds. The aim is to keep the mind focused on the specific tone or "beats" that is being played.

Affirmation meditation. This meditative

technique uses affirmations to plant a certain way of thinking or generate particular feelings within a practitioner's mind. You will get into a relaxed mental state, and the idea is that one is often more suggestive when relaxed; the message is received and sinks in better to your brain. During affirmative relaxation, positive affirmations linked or connected to a specific area, such as health, relaxation, mood, and confidence will be stated.

Every time you want to embark on a relaxation technique, do the following:

- Find a quiet spot where you will not be disturbed.

- Get into a comfortable position, sitting or lying down.

- Loosen your clothes and free your arms and legs.

- Dim your lights.

Mastering these relaxation techniques will take time. Over time, your body will be in tune with the sequence of the relaxation techniques. With this mastery, you will be able to get deeper relaxation. Make these practices part of your lifestyle, and do them daily. As much as it may be difficult to find exclusive time for meditation, these techniques can be put into practice as you engage in doing other things.

It is possible to meditate on a bus or while commuting for concentrative meditation. Mindfulness techniques can be put into play while walking or exercising your pet or while taking a lunch break at the park. Nonetheless, if you can designate a daily time for relaxation, do so for predictability and ease. Do not try these relaxation techniques while sleepy as you will fall asleep and miss out on your target for relaxation. Relaxation requires maximum concentration and alertness.

No one is perfect, especially at the beginning. Do not pinch yourself for missing some sessions. The main goal is to build momentum so that after a while you can get into a rhythm and routine.

Peace of Mind

Peace of mind is the key to a true life. Happiness, good health, and success are things that should be accessed by every one of us. Meditation is one of the ways that you can do to attain the mental peace that will give you a wholesome life. When we look at the many benefits of meditative practices listed earlier, they refer or are a testament to a state where one's body is in total control and fully functional.

Bad habits are jettisoned for more pure, health-conscious ones. Mental strength and brain functioning are greatly improved and nurtured. Immunity is boosted, leading to fewer or no diseases affecting us. We are less stressed and a lot happier when we meditate regularly. This happiness and well-being are what spawn peace of mind. One becomes aware and in tune with themselves. Full self-awareness is achieved, and with that comes the peace. When your mind is peaceful, you will be more productive. You will relate better with people around you. Your family, friends, colleagues at work, and strangers that you bump into will notice the difference in how you relate. You become more likable as the happiness and peace you exude rubs off onto others.

Meditation, indeed, leads to peace of mind. Take up meditation, won't you?

Quick and Simple Techniques for a Beginner's Practice

Now that you have all the basic knowledge you need, it is time to delve into the practice itself. There are many kinds of meditation techniques that you can get acquainted with, and this chapter will aim to give you as many options as possible to help you start strong.

Fast and Simple: Techniques on the Go

There are just too many people out there who don't have enough time in their hands but still want to practice meditation. Although meditation can be done anywhere and in almost any circumstance, it is important that you start with some beginner-friendly practices that won't take up too much time. All the exercises in this section can be done within ten minutes, but you can make it last longer if you want.

When you are using certain techniques to fit a certain time frame, you have to put all thought of time constraints out of your head. It would be best if you chose a short time after you wake up or just before you go to bed. Keep in mind that making your mind be still is not easily accomplished, especially for a beginner. But also know that this can become simpler and easier as you go along, so don't let yourself be discouraged by any short-term setbacks.

Basic Meditation with Affirmation

This basic meditation technique is a great way to start your practice. This starts off with the basics, and you can add visualizations or added stillness later on.

- Sit on the floor or on a chair, and keep your back as straight as possible without straining yourself. Make sure that you are comfortable and can hold the position for at least five minutes. Choose a place where you won't be disturbed.

- Breathe deeply and relax your body as you breathe. As this is probably your first time, it might be wise to keep your eyes closed throughout the process.

- Choose a phrase that you would like to affirm in your life. Try to use the first person, and make sure it's something meaningful to you. Examples can include the following: "There is peace inside me," "I am worthy of love," or "God watches over me."

- Take slow measured breaths. Make your breathing as easy and relaxed as possible, and empty your mind of other thoughts.

- Now repeat the affirmation to yourself quietly. Try to focus only on the affirmation. If you do get distracted by random thoughts, allow the thought to pass rather than suppress it. Simply return your attention to the affirmation gently.

- If you find it difficult to focus with a purely mental effort, you can try to whisper the words to yourself, moving your tongue without really speaking a word. Join your breathing with your affirmation and repeat the phrase as you breathe out.

Continue this exercise for at least five minutes. Remember not to get frustrated as your body will end up tensing rather than relaxing. Notice how you felt during the exercise. Was focusing your attention on affirmations and breathing difficult for you? What kinds of thoughts did you find popping into your head?

Focused Breathing

When you can manage to stay focused on affirmations, it is time you focus solely on the breath. This is a great way to develop focused awareness, concentration, and stillness of the mind. Don't expect to have a quiet mind right away. This is all normal and will improve as you continue your practice.

- Sit comfortably with your back straight in a place where you won't be disturbed.

- Breathe deeply and relax your body. You can choose to close your eyes or keep them open. However, if you find that your thoughts still have a tendency to race around you, keeping your eyes closed will help keep distractions at the minimal.

- Turn your attention toward the sensation of your breath. This is a good time to practice the beginner's mind. Experience your breathing as if for the first time. Feel your chest rise and fall as you breathe. Listen intently to the sound of each breath, and feel the air enter and leave your body.

- Continue this meditation for at least five minutes. Since you are focusing solely on your breathing, you might find yourself easily distracted by random thoughts and emotions. Don't be alarmed or critical of yourself when this happens. Simply acknowledge the thought or emotion without judgment, then let it go. Gently direct your focus back to your breathing.

It would be beneficial for you to continue practicing these techniques before you move on to more complex practices. As the basic core of almost all the meditation practices involves awareness of the breath and concentration, these techniques are great if you simply want to stay with the basics or if you want to move on and deepen your practice.

Rolling Up Your Sleeves: Longer and Deeper Practices

You can liken your mind to a deep lake. If you only look at the surface (the ordinary mind), you're often blind to the wonders underneath. When you start practicing focused awareness, you're actually learning to swim in the waters of your own mind. Once you start getting better at swimming, then you can start diving deeper into the depths. This section will introduce more intermediate practices that allow you to get a good look into your own psyche. The exercises in this section should be done for twenty minutes or more. You can extend the length of your practice according to your own preference and needs.

Body-Tuning Technique

This technique is one of the most important intermediate techniques in meditation as it gets you back in touch with your body. A great majority of people in society are fragmented. The mind is often torn in fragments of positive and negative emotions that aren't fully explored. Worst of all, the body is disconnected from awareness and the mind. This technique aims to get the mind and body reconnected to make them whole again.

- This meditation must be done lying down. Find a flat, solid surface that allows for comfort but not so much that you can end up drifting off to sleep.

- Direct your awareness to your body as a whole. Pay attention to every sensation that you feel. Feel the places where your body touches the surface of where you're lying on. Feel the cool breeze that wafts through the room or the warmth of your own body.

- After a few minutes of full-body awareness, gently direct your attention toward the biggest toe of your left foot. Feel all the sensations in this one area. If you don't feel anything, then simply focus on the lack of sensation.

- Start visualizing your breath flow in and out of your toe, bringing the much-needed energy with it. When you're ready, expand your awareness toward your whole left foot and continue to breathe in and out of it. Continue this for at least two minutes.

- Once you're done, let your awareness travel upward to your ankles and lower leg. Be patient with yourself and continue visualizing your breath going in and out in waves across this area of your body.

- From here, go up to your knees and thighs. When you're done with your left leg, go back down and focus on your right fight. Repeat the visualization and focus on your other foot. From here, continue to go higher. From the pelvis, go higher to the abdomen, lower back, the navel, upper back, then the chest and shoulders.

- Try to slow down in the areas where there are main organs, such as the lungs, heart, and stomach. Imagine your breath bringing healing energy to your organs. Now bring your focus to your left fingers and hands then up toward your elbows and arms. Repeat the same technique until you've finished with both hands.

From here, bring your awareness to your neck, then up to your face. Give special attention to the space right between your brows. Finally, finish by focusing on the top of your head. The last two areas can be especially receptive. You might end up feeling like you're floating and that your consciousness is more fluid in your own body.

- When you're ready, pull your awareness away from your head, and bring your awareness back to your whole body. Feel your breath go in and out in waves.

- After a few minutes, wriggle your toes and fingers and slowly open your hand. Return your awareness to normal and stretch a little before you get up.

Meditation with Visualizations

Visualizations can be added to your basic meditation techniques and can help develop a certain trait or attitude in you. When practicing certain visualization techniques, simply start off with basic breathing meditation. When you feel at peace and still, you can start your visualization.

The Sanctuary

Visualizing a sanctuary or a refuge is a great place to recharge your energy and shake off some stress and anxiety. This technique can also help in healing certain mental and emotional wounds.

- Do your standard, basic meditation until your mind is relatively still and your body relaxed (preferably for five minutes).

- Start visualizing a place where you've always felt safe. It might be a real place from your past or just something you imagined. As long as it makes you feel safe and protected, then it should work. Be as specific as you want. If you imagine yourself in a garden then what plants can be found there? Are there singing birds and trees that provide shade? Do your best to make the visualization as vivid as possible.

- Once you've found your safe place, simply allow the sensation of peacefulness, safety, and comfort permeate across your entire being. Know that you are safe here and that no one can touch you here. Within your sanctuary, you can explore all your emotions, even those of hurt, fear, and humiliation.

- Stay in your sanctuary for as long as you need and make sure to end your session by reaffirming the positive emotions you feel in your safe place.

Mindfulness Anytime, Anywhere

Mindfulness meditation can be done at any time while doing other things. This makes mindfulness one of the best ways to do meditation on the go. As long as you completely pay attention to what you're doing in the present. You have to be able to combine focused awareness with welcoming acceptance. The aim of mindfulness meditation is to have you fully present in whatever you're doing.

Mindful Eating

This is a great mindfulness exercise that you can do at

work during your lunch break. Simply find a quiet place and eat your lunch.

- Appreciate your food as you lay it out in front of you. Think of the effort and hard work that's gone into making your meal.

- Look and smell. Note the appearance and aroma of your food. Be curious and notice everything you can see and smell.

- Bring the food to your lips and note how it feels against your tongue. Savor the taste of the food as you chew. Take note of all the emotions you feel as you eat.

- Try to stay mindful throughout the entire meal.

Mindfulness can be done along with any other chores and activities as long as you practice focused attention. You can be mindful as you walk down a street or as you clean up around the house. You can even be mindful while talking to a friend or spending time with your family. Mindfulness can only amplify the joy and satisfaction that you feel as you engage in these activities.

Tips to Take It All the Way

You now have everything you need to start a practice, but what if you hit a few snags along the way? This section is about some user-friendly tips to help make your practice work for you. This section is about all the little things you need to keep in mind to have a successful practice. After all, God is in the details.

- Position: There are three basic positions you can take when meditating—namely, lying down, sitting up on a chair, or kneeling on the floor. Make sure to extend your spine as much as possible.

  o *Lying down.* Lie down with your feet hip-width apart and let your feet fall naturally. You can place small cushions under your neck and knees for comfort.

  o *Sitting up on a chair.* It is important not to slouch or lean against your chair. Make sure that your buttocks sit a little higher than your knees so that your pelvis can naturally tilt forward. It is best if you use an old-fashioned, wooden chair or bench.

  o *Kneeling.* This is considered to be the optimal meditation position. Because you are so close to the ground, you can become more in tune with the energies of nature and the earth, and it is also the most stable position. However, it can be more difficult as it does take more flexibility and muscle strength. Research positions before you start if you want to consider kneeling. Try basic positions, such as the easy kneeling position and the Burmese position, before moving to the lotus position.

- Clothing: There are no special clothes you need to wear. You just have to make sure your clothes are comfortable and not too tight. Make sure what you wear won't distract you in any way.

- Location: Make sure the place where you meditate can accommodate the amount of time you need to finish your practice. Avoid places in the house that have a lot of "traffic," such as the kitchen, living room, and dining room. Eventually, you might want to create a special space with a meditation altar. This altar does not have to be associated with a certain faith or religion but simply hold all the items that are special to you. It can have incense, flowers, rocks you found in nature, and even pictures of your inspirations.

- When: Basically, you can meditate whenever you have spare time. The best time for morning people is an hour right after you wake up. Being refreshed can help you be more focused and still than any other time.

For those who aren't morning people, however, right after work or before bed is also good options as they can help relax you. The downside, though, is that you might already be distracted and exhausted from the events of the day. If you have the space, you can also try meditating during your lunch break if you find that any other time is not possible.

Quick Tips That Can Make Meditation Easier

- Star with the basics: Becoming too ambitious on your first try can leave you feeling overwhelmed. Try a five-minute basic meditation before you start doing a body-tuning technique just to test the waters first.

- Start within your comfort zone: Distractions can be your worst enemy when starting out, and doing a kneeling position that leaves you numb won't help. Start in a place, position, and time that are most comfortable with you. You don't have to follow the guidelines strictly if it causes pain. Be lenient and patient with yourself. If a position is painful, try a different one. Eventually, with a few stretches every day, you will be able to do even the full lotus.

Distracting aches and itches: It can be hard to maintain a certain position if you know you have to stay still. Feeling little itches and aches can pop up when you still your mind. The best way to deal with this is to be fully aware of the sensation. As you explore the sensation with curiosity and acceptance, you will find these little discomforts fade away. This is why meditation is often used as therapy for those who suffer chronic pain.

Chapter Four:

How to Deal with Stress to Get Rid of Anxiety

Run the Stress Off

Running is a great way of combating stress. It is one of the easiest and beneficial physical exercises anyone can engage in. If you are feeling beat down by the rigors of life, take a run down your street or get to the nearest field and run a few laps. There are several benefits that you will experience if you run regularly:

- *Running being an aerobic exercise.* This increases the heart rate and makes you sweat, stimulates the release of endorphins, which are the body's natural feel-good chemicals, leaving your brain elated, and making you happy.

- You will shed calories, which will help with lowering your blood pressure and keeping your arteries in good shape.

- Running slows the aging process and reduces bone and muscle loss by building strength and flexibility. It keeps you active and improves your overall health.

- When running, you have all the time to yourself, which allows you to process your thoughts. You may use the time to aid you with sorting out some issues that you may be facing or to think through a problem.

- Researchers have found out that people who are regular runners lead a happier, more stress-free life and are generally fitter than those who do not. Your concentration and alertness are also enhanced.

Now, put on those running shoes and hit the road for a healthier, happier, and stress-free life. Running can be done almost anywhere you go. You do not have to worry about where to perform this exercise. It is recommended that you drink a lot of water if you are a runner. Drink at least a liter of water an hour to two hours before your run. This helps with the hydration of the body, and you are unlikely to suffer dehydration.

You will not regret your decision as the benefits that will accrue to you are many.

Take a Hike

Hiking is a relaxing walk through natural surroundings, usually at a nature trail, a park, or a forest. Much like running, hiking is a great exercise for stress relief, though less vigorous. Hiking combines the benefits of an effective aerobic exercise, serene natural surroundings, and the chance and time to relax and think freely.

The following are ways by which hiking helps the body to deal with stress:

Mental Relaxation

Hiking provides the time and opportunity for mind relaxation by getting you up close to nature. Nature has been proven as a catalyst to mental relaxation by giving you the experience and wonders of natural surroundings.

Energizing the Body

Hiking being an aerobic exercise invigorates the body and helps with the regulation of stress chemicals. People who hike regularly have higher levels of feel-good hormones, like endorphins, which reduce stress considerably.

Emotional Well-Being

When you are stressed, you are a prisoner of negative emotions, like sadness, anxiety, nervousness, etc. Hiking will activate positive energy in your body, which will, in turn, boost your emotions to make you feel better and happier.

Brain Exercising

A hike will afford you the silence and time to think profoundly about things that are important to you. Aerobic exercise coupled with deep thinking will effectively enhance the body's stress management capabilities.

Spiritual Nourishment

Being in a natural environment with the wonderful serenity offers the body a chance to get spiritually fulfilled. Your nerves will be calmed, and you will get the opportunity for mental clarity and relaxation that you would normally not have every day. Hiking is a great exercise for anxiety and stress relief, and you ought to prepare in advance before you go on a hike. Pack a first-aid kit, drinking water, and a phone in case you may be confronted with an accident.

Come on, why don't you start hiking for a change? It

may just be the answer to dealing with the stress you have been under lately. So book an appointment with nature for exercise, mental and spiritual fulfillment, and say goodbye to stress and anxiety.

Pedal the Stress Away

Do you remember how happy you were riding your bicycle when you were young? I remember my experience, and I could give anything to feel the same way again—excited, happy, and with a sense of unbridled freedom. It was just a great time without a care in the world. Well, you do not have to look back to your childhood with such nostalgia because you can readily bring back those feel-good moments you had on your bicycle then to the present to replace all the anxiety and worries you are facing now!

Don't you want to?

Cycling is another form of aerobic exercise, which is great for stress relief, fitness, and general well-being. When you are overwhelmed by life's pressures, simply hop on a bike and start pedaling for stress relief. Being on the bike will take your mind off the problems that are bothering you, pump some feel-good chemicals into your bloodstream, and pace your heart to leave you feeling refreshed and emotionally elated.

You can cycle after work, on weekends, or your day off. You can even cycle to work. While doing this, employ the meditative technique of mantra by chanting a positive phrase or word to the rhythm of your pedaling. I assure you that you will be surprised at how fast your mind will be cleared of the negativity and stress that you are facing.

Cycling is not an expensive endeavor. Just buy a bicycle, and you may start. It is not vigorous if done for leisure or exercise and can be taken up by people of all ages. Cycling will keep you fit. Work out your heart for better health and emotional balance. It helps with the management of chronic conditions, like diabetes, cardiovascular problems, and high blood pressure. The healthier and better you feel, the less likely you are to be stressed. Get on your bike, and enjoy the stress-relieving benefits you have been missing.

Reading for Stress Relief

Reading is cathartic and is a great reliever of stress for people who are facing everyday pressures and adversity by relaxing the brain and managing the thought process. When you read, your mind travels away from the pressures you are facing. You sink into the story where you will find yourself in faraway worlds. In the duration of your reading, you shall be transported away from your troubles, and this helps in balancing your emotional well-being.

Reading is a great mental exercise that stimulates brain activity, thereby improving mental concentration and alertness. Stress-fighting chemicals that give you a happy feeling are released into the brain. An active mind is strong and more likely to cope with daily pressures. You will also fight stress from the motivation and hope you derive from reading biographies and motivational books. Books and other literature are sources of information that enables you to learn more and aid in problem-solving.

A book will divert your thoughts from the lingering problems or worries that are stressing you out. Set aside a few hours in your day to read, and you will experience how fulfilling it can be in your efforts at dealing with stress.

When you clear your mind of negativity even for a few hours, you will make huge strides in mental relaxation. With a relaxed mind, you should be able to be more creative and relaxed enabling you to cope with stress. An active mind also slows down the aging process, leaving you feeling younger physically and mentally. A strong, healthy body is less prone to stress.

If the last time you read was for an exam or for a school assignment, make a hot cup of tea, make yourself comfortable on your favorite seat, and immerse yourself into a book. The benefits for your life and health are great—you need to try it. Get literature that appeals to you—a book, magazine, or newspaper—and make it a habit to read regularly for a less stressful life every day.

Be a Positive Thinker

Have you heard of *positive thinking*? Well, the world works in a very simple way in that whatever you think is what will be manifested in your life. You attract what you think! It may seem simplistic or difficult to accept, but take the time to mull it over and you realize that it is true. If you want to get that new job you applied to or want to get promoted, it begins by you wanting it then believing that you can get it without having a shred of doubt.

Self-belief is a powerful stress reliever. To always be positive and to be ever optimistic. The power of positive thinking is incredible. If you look forward to good things, you will have a happier, less stressful life. Positive thinking is a state where you look forward to favorable outcomes in whatever you do. Positive thinking, therefore, involves actively training your mind to have creative thoughts that transform energy into reality.

Avoid dwelling on your failures and concentrate on the successes. Use the disappointments as lessons for the future. Studies show that positive thinking leads to a longer and healthier life since you are less prone to stress. You become a positive thinker by identifying the negative aspects of your thinking and avoid them while constantly evaluation your thoughts to make sure you stay on the positive.

Do not be too hard on yourself, allow yourself joyous moments and take time to have fun. Surround yourself with like-minded people who will help you build the habit of positive thinking. When you are optimistic, you become less critical and are instead more creative and hopeful. An optimistic mindset is able to deal with stress at work more easily and constructively. Positive thinking is a powerful tool in fighting stress and anxiety. Try it, and you are sure of great benefits and a happy, relaxed life.

Time Management

If you are always late and short of time, then you are most likely leading a stressed and anxious life. There is nothing as stressful as the struggle to always meet a deadline or catch up with something you forgot about. Using the little time we have properly will help you cope with stress. Time management involves methods aimed at using time efficiently to perform all the tasks we have within a given time. It involves prioritizing, scheduling, and organizing.

You must assess the tasks on your plate and put them in order of importance and urgency to avoid confusion, conflicts, and unnecessary time pressures. Plan things in advance to avoid last-minute scrambling in an effort to get something that skipped your mind done. Good time management makes you a more productive person. You will do more within a short time, thus gaining more control of your life.

Create a schedule and stick to it. You will have enough free time to engage in fun things that you have been missing. You will have time to go to the movies, play a game or any other fun activity that serves to boost health and well-being. Good time management means that you have enough time for work, family, and friends. These moments with loved ones are most fulfilling and stress-relieving.

It does not take much to be a good time manager. All you need is to start and commit to it. Well-managed time leads to a more comfortable and happy life. Below are the benefits of time management for a less stressful life:

- doing more with less time

- getting more free time, which allows time to relax

- reduced stress since you do not worry about pending deadlines

- higher productivity since you are fresh mentally, physically and highly motivated

Time management is good because you will be happier, more successful, and more productive. You will also live a fuller and stress-free life. Why don't you start managing your time better and enjoy the benefits?

Get Enough Sleep

Are you sleeping enough? Lack of adequate sleep is a big contributor to incidences of stress and anxiety. Getting sufficient sleep is essential in your effort to deal with stress. During sleep, your body gets the chance to rest, to heal, and to be rejuvenated. When you do not get enough sleep, you are left susceptible to stress and other health problems because you are emotionally imbalanced.

Therefore, it is imperative to have a sleeping schedule and follow it so that you condition your body into a routine for sufficient rest. In fact, sleep deficiency is a great source of stress and anxiety since you are tired, irritable, and have weakened creativity. Between work and your personal affairs, you probably end up not getting enough sleep. It is recommended that you sleep for at least six hours for optimal rest. However, many of us do not meet this target as studies show that most of us sleep for as little as two hours and a maximum of four hours in a twenty-four-hour cycle!

We do not get sufficient sleep because of our poor bedtime habits that end up interfering with our sleep. To sleep better and longer, try the following:

- Set a sleeping schedule. You will sleep better if your bedtime is predictable. Your body will adapt, and you will rest more.

- Do not indulge in a heavy meal during dinner. Have a light meal at least two hours before you retire to bed.

- Physical exercise is a great sleep inducer. Work out three to four hours before you sleep.

- Do not take caffeinated drinks close to your bedtime. Your last caffeine drink should be averagely six hours or more before you lie down.

- Keep away from alcohol four to six hours before your bedtime. It will disrupt your sleep.

Sleep well for emotional balance. You will wake up refreshed, well-rested, and energized. When your body has this balance, it can easily manage or ward off stress.

Listening to Soothing Music

Music is very relaxing and has the ability to change moods positively by acting on our minds to avert stress. It acts quickly, is available, and will relieve you of stress and anxiety. The calming effect of music has a distinctive relationship to our emotions and is an effective way to cope with stress. Slow classical music is extremely peaceful and has a positive effect on our bodies and minds. This kind of music has its advantages. It slows the heart and pulse rates and reduces the production of stress hormones and blood pressure.

Music engrosses our thoughts to distract us from whatever worries may be lingering in our minds. Most times, when you are stressed and anxious, your mind tends to wander off, causing you to think of the things that cause you more anxiety. However, music acts as a cushion and helps your mind to relax and better concentrate.

For years, music has been proven to treat ailments and restore coherence and balance between your body and mind. Furthermore, research has it that music is therapeutic in the following ways:

- Some music compositions can help disabled people by boosting harmonization and communication and improve their life.

- The use of headphones when listening to music can lessen anxiety and stress, especially when one is about to go for surgery and after the surgery.

- During extreme pain or post-surgery, music has been known to ease and numb the pain.

- Music is also known to alleviate depression and enhance self-esteem in older people.

- Soothing music has been proven to improve mood and reduce burnout.

- Music is therapeutic, especially for cancer patients, as it improves the quality of life and reduces emotional trauma.

Music is food for the soul. The next time you are facing adversity or are feeling down from mental fatigue or some other worries, turn on your favorite music. Enjoy the relaxing and positive vibes that will be provided by the music.

Share Your Problems by Talking to Someone

A problem shared is a problem solved or half solved. How insightful this is. Sharing our problems is therapeutic and a quick fix to stress. Putting a lid on your suffering and keeping it to yourself is an emotional burden and is very unhealthy. Many of us are fiercely independent and would want to solve our problems on our own. However, there is a point where you are better off talking to someone about what you are going through.

Pent-up emotions and suffering will turn you into a very stressed and imbalanced person. Reach out to someone you trust—a friend or relative—for a listening ear and realize the great positive impact it will have on you. Talking to someone has the following benefits:

- Sharing your problems will help you get rid of bad emotions, like worries, anxiety, etc. You will feel better after since you will have let go of the emotional burden.

- Your pain is reduced since you will have someone sharing your problem and empathizing with you.

- Solutions to your problems are easier to come by as you will be readily advised by the listener.

- By sharing, you lead a healthier life since you negate the effects of emotional distress caused by pent-up emotional turmoil.

- You will simply feel better and happier at having talked about whatever is bothering you.

By sharing, we get the load off our chests, leaving us

emotionally boosted, relaxed, and stronger. It also prevents the situation from deteriorating to a much-deeper problem, like depression or emotional breakdown. With a relaxed and more stable mental state, you have the clarity and strength to handle your problem, and you will easily embark on problem-solving for a stress-free life.

From now on, if you find yourself in a tight place emotionally and are feeling stressed, seek someone you can share your problem with and enjoy the quick stress relief that comes with it.

You Should Laugh More

The benefits of laughter in coping with stress and for a healthier life are numerous. It is proven that humor is a powerful tool for stress relief. Try to laugh and be cheerful despite the tough times. Laughter has a way of rubbing off on others, so if you are happy, those around you will follow, and you will be surrounded by happiness. A happy life is a stress-free life.

Laughter enhances oxygen intake and stimulates the functioning of body organs, like the heart, brain, and lungs. Your heart rate is also improved for better blood flow and cardiovascular well-being. By laughing your way through life, you benefit from muscles' relaxation and tension relief. Your immunity will be enhanced through the release of stress-fighting chemicals in the body. All the pain you are suffering emotionally and even physically is reduced by laughter, which triggers the production of the body's natural pain-killing hormones.

A happy person is a magnet, attracting people for improved social life and emotional state. So when you are downcast, just smile through it; you will feel better. In any case, the difficulties will soon pass; and with a positive and happy approach, you will survive it. Laughter subdues toxic stress-attracting thoughts. It helps you forget your worries and enables you to concentrate and work on the tasks at hand. Be happy and grateful for the good things you have been blessed with. Think about them when you are stressed. Laugh and smile as you recollect, and be assured of a stress-free life.

A good sense of humor is not a panacea, but it is sure to improve your outlook in life, your health, and your social standing. A good laugh will do you a lot of good. Smile and laugh more. Laughter is, indeed, the best medicine.

Eat Healthy Foods

Food is the fuel and the source of nourishment for the body, an integral part of our general well-being and good health. It is important that we eat the right foods and eat well for us to stay healthy. A healthy body is able to fend off the side effects of stress with ease.

Food and stress are uniquely interwoven. When faced with adversity, some people have a sudden craving for food while others will lose their appetite. It is, therefore, necessary that we know the right foods to eat, especially when we are under some sort of stress. When we encounter stress, we crave comfort foods, such as fats and sugars. These foods are not healthy and cause harm to us and will cause us more stress. To stay healthy and manage stress, we have to avoid the following:

- *Consumption of a lot of fast foods.* They are unhealthy and more expensive than cooking for yourself in the long run.

- *Skipping meals.* It is a catalyst for stress. If you miss meals, you are likely to be fatigued and less nourished, thus susceptible to stress.

- *Drinking too many caffeinated drinks.* This interferes with your sleep and denies you adequate rest.

- *Eating wrong food types.* Eat a balanced diet and resist the temptation of eating too much of foods rich in fats and sugars. These foods only lead to weight gain and cardiovascular problems.

A poor diet will leave you with problems of hormonal imbalance and weight problems—either loss or too much gain. You will develop a weak immune system and are likely to be susceptible to illnesses. Unhealthy eating will also lead to an imbalance of the blood sugar, which may lead to diabetes. Stress makes your body burn nutrients. You consume much faster than normal; that is why you should be on a healthy diet. It is wise that you replenish these nutrients to help cope with stress.

Work-Life Balance

"All work with no play makes Jack a dull boy!" This old saying is very true. You need to have some time away from your job to have fun and engage in things that excite you and pump your blood. Most adults who are stressed can trace the source to their workplace because we spend a lot of time on the job. It is, therefore, important to balance the time we spend working and time for ourselves for a healthier lifestyle.

Work-life balance is about dividing your time effectively and adequately between work and your private life. If you let work consume most of your time, you neglect or shortchange your personal needs, and you will end up stressed. When your personal life is in order, you are less likely to be stressed since you will worry less. Your mind will not be stretched from being divided between what you need to do at work and the personal matters awaiting your attention.

Spend time with family and friends. It is relaxing and healthy for you. When was the last time you went cycling or shopping with your children? These mundane activities are the foundation to a well-balanced, healthy life devoid of stress. If your private life brings you happiness, you will be able to face pressures that come your way. After spending time with your loved ones, you need to set aside personal time for things that are self-gratifying. Go for a massage or run a few laps at the neighborhood field. Volunteer your services for a worthy cause. Such acts are great for boosting your emotional well-being.

If you embrace a healthy work-life balance, you will reap the many benefits. Personal nourishment and care are important for overall health. Balance your private and professional life for a stress-free, healthy life where you are happier and revitalized.

Pick Up Your Pen and Paper and Write

Another technique of dealing with stress is writing. It is especially encouraged when one is so stressed or depressed. Putting down your experience, feelings, and thoughts in a journal is very therapeutic for recovery and for defeating stress. Writing works by clarifying your mind and thoughts, and it is a form of therapy in the sense that it compels you to recall events and thoughts of the day on paper to give you a better avenue to analyze and understand what happened. It is also meditative. It slows down your heart as you focus on your writing to stream out your thoughts to paper.

Writing sharpens and stimulates brain functioning and activity to improve your mental acuity and concentration. It also improves your vocabulary. You are, therefore, better equipped to handle stressful situations. When you write regularly, the stress triggers in your head are disrupted, allowing you to relax and sleep better. You get up well rested and energized. Writing also fights anger by removing the thoughts from your mind to the writing pad, essentially offering you a platform to vent it out.

When you write down your worries and problems, it is easier to solve them. Writing allows you to identify what the problem is. Think it through over time and most likely come up with a great unrushed solution and avert the stress that you may have. Having a to-do list or schedule helps you focus and get organized. You are able to plan in advance to avoid last-minute rushes or procrastination, which will only serve to make your life stressful.

Writing will boost your immune system; by slowing your breathing, you are able to breathe in more oxygen to better nourish the brain and blood, leading to faster healing and an enhanced ability to fight pathogens. Better breathing also strengthens the lungs, which has a positive effect in fighting respiratory conditions, like asthma. To reap the benefits of writing for better health and stress relief, it does not matter what you write. The main thing is to be able to jot down your thoughts and review them. You do not have to be a John Grisham! Write down what is on your mind because the healing power lies in you letting out the negative thoughts that are weighing on your mind.

Are you happy with your life right now? What would make you happy? Do you have a plan for getting it? Would you like some help? I might be able to help you. Are you be interested? Sign up for my newsletter. I give out a free workbook to help with social anxiety issues so those who sign up. I am also writing more books and posting articles that can help deal with other issues related to social anxiety. There's also a community that I'm building for people who are going through similar issues as you. If it's okay with you, I'd also like to get your feedback so I can write more about things that could help you. Does that sound like something that might help you? I hope it does, because I really want to help. I have been in your shoes before so I know how it feels. Join my newsletter and let's all help each other. Does that sound good? Visit my website now at **http://jen.green** and join my newsletter!

Chapter Five:

When Social Anxiety Strikes

Back

In this chapter, we shall discuss ways and ideas of preventing lapses and relapses.

Practicing without Giving Up

The best way to prevent a relapse is to keep practicing your CBT skills. In case you are regularly practicing, you will be in a good position to handle whatever situations you are confronted with. Come up with a plan for yourself of what skills you are going to work on every week. This might include direct exposure or practicing some relaxed breathing and relaxation. You can involve and ask your family and friends to help.

Being Aware of Your Red Flags

You happen to be less likely to have a relapse once you know when you are more vulnerable to having one. For instances, several relapses happen during the times that we are under stress or when going through some changes. Make a directory of indicators that tell you when your anxiety might be increasing. This list might include the following:

- more feelings of panic

- improved tasks at home or at work

- a lot more anxious ideas

- arguments with loved ones

- major life changes, such as weddings, childbirth, or death within the family

- avoiding more activities

Make a plan of action. Once you really know what your red flags or danger signs are, you can make a plan for how to cope with them. This might include the following:

- practicing your CBT skills more often

- taking some time on your own

- relaxing by reading a book, shopping or speaking to a friend

Coming Up with New Challenges

Like everyone else on this earth, you will always be a work in progress. This means there will always be something you can do to improve yourself and make your life more enjoyable and fulfilling. A good way to prevent future relapses is to continue working on new challenges and new feared situations. You can make a listing of situations that are still scary or bring you anxiety, and work on them over time. You are highly unlikely to slip back to your old ways if you are always working towards being victorious over your anxiety.

Learning from Your Relapses

Keep in mind that it is normal to occasionally have relapses. In our lives, everyone goes through episodes of stress, and in case you are experiencing anxiety, you have higher chances of a relapse. The beauty of it is that you can learn so much from your relapses. Try to analyze what it is that led to you to suffer from a relapse by asking yourself the following questions:

- Were you having upsetting or anxious thoughts?

- Was your anxiety very high?

- Did you do something different?

- Were you aware that the situation would be

difficult, or you were taken by surprise?

Knowing why a situation proved difficult for you can assist in preparing for the next time it occurs. You can come up with a plan that would assist you to cope more comfortably when in tough situations in the future.

Getting acquainted with the reality

It is a fact that how you speak to your inner-self after a relapse has a huge impact on your behavior later on. If you believe that you are good for nothing and have destroyed all your hard labor, you will likely throw in the towel, quit trying, and finish up relapsing. But here are a few facts:

- It is not possible to go back to where you began. You can't just decide to forget all the skills and methods that you were taught by CBT. Going back to where it all began simply means going through anxiety and having no idea how to handle it. But after you have started using CBT, you *do know* how to handle your anxiety.

- In case you experience a relapse, you have the ability to pick yourself up and get back on track. It might have taken you a number of weeks or several months of practice to reduce your symptoms of anxiety; however, it won't take you that long to get back to where you were before the relapse. When you get back to practicing your CBT skills, you will be mastering your anxiety again in no time.

Being Kind to Yourself

It is very important to remember that relapses are nothing out of the ordinary. Desist being hard on yourself, because this doesn't help. It is far more useful to realize that we all make mistakes sometimes. All of us don't speak to others in such a simply way; therefore, it is obviously a bad idea to speak to our inner-selves in this manner. In truth, it can, in fact, be helpful to have a relapse since it gives you a possibility to learn that relapses are normal and that relapses can be conquered if you go back to involving your skills. Ensure that you are patient with yourself. Study from your lapses and move ahead.

Honoring Yourself

Ensure that you always honor yourself for all the hard labor you put into being better. It is very encouraging to treat yourself at times. A bonus might be heading out for a good meal, buying yourself something totally new, going out with friends, or perhaps spending time relaxing, enjoying, and pampering yourself. Never forget that anxiety management is not an easy job, and any kind of improvement you make is because of your own attempts. Doesn't that deserve an incentive?

If you're not prepared for anxiety relapses, you may fall into a relapse, which can leave you feeling helpless, guilty, and embarrassed. It can be difficult to pick yourself up from the relapse, yet take into account that you can study from these experiences. Moving forward, it's important that will you know how to prevent relapses and look for treatment as necessary.

Conclusion

We have gone through the definition, causes, and remedies of social anxiety. This book has offered easy-to-use but very powerful and effective techniques for tackling social anxiety for you to have a transformation in your life that will bring you harmony and happiness. You have also read a little about my own story and how I can now help others through my experiences.

You are now familiar with what social anxiety is and its profound powers over a person's life. You should also be in a position to appreciate the principle that positive thoughts attract positive results, and conversely, negative mental images will only serve to bring more negativity into your life. You have also learned that you have the power to create your life and that your thoughts will create the life you live.

For this book to work for you, it is vital that you encompass all the advice and techniques you have read herein. It may not be in the order that I listed them in this book, but you must use all of them for maximum benefits.

You are now aware that you must know and decide to overcome social anxiety and write down what you desire your life to be like. The next thing you would want to do is put in a request for what you want. Believe in what you want and have settled on is important, and you should not allow any doubts to creep in after.

The power of meditation and visualization should now be very clear, and the importance cannot be stressed more than I have. Just as important is the ability to own what you desire in the abstract. Have faith that it is yours even before you receive it. Talking about what you want is another important technique that you must apply for total success over anxiety. Talk about your desires with friends and relatives. Share your dreams, and by so doing, you will be sending the right signals to attract the life you want even faster.

Always think about what you want and engage in positive thoughts. Any negative thoughts will chip away on the progress you have made. Last but not least, you also now know the power of gratitude. Always be thankful for everything in your life. More importantly, remember that for the transformation to work, you must work and act toward your desired goals. There are no miracles.

Start now and start by making small steps that will allow you to effectively use the techniques to your advantage. Have no doubt whatsoever because overcoming social anxiety to transforming lives is proven; it is up to you to pick the area of your life or what you want and put in the request to the universe to begin the process of transformation. Make further inquiries and do further research to widen your knowledge about social anxiety as well as the techniques herein.

For this book to be effective, you have to be a clear thinker. You need to nurture habits that will help you achieve your desire for clarity of thought, leaving you healthier, happier, and more successful. It is through clear thinking that you will achieve success, happiness, personal fulfillment, and good health.

You are what you think!

When you cannot think clearly, you often make regrettable decisions. Anxiety sets in because you are constantly unsure or worried and the consequential stress leads to poor health. Indeed, clear thinking is critical for personal well-being and health.

You need to learn how to improve your health for better mental clarity by nurturing the strengths that are already in your possession and by adjusting some areas of your life that cloud your judgment. Clear thinking has been defined as not being confused and having the ability to think clearly and intelligently. It is being clear-headed. Clear thinking, in my view, is to have the presence of mind to effectively manage your thoughts, analyze the thoughts, and make sound decisions at the end.

For you to be a clear thinker, you need the ability to process thought rationally and in detail through independent and introspective thinking. It is more than an acquisition of information as it is not singularly dependent on memory. You must be capable of preempting consequences from what you know for greater knowledge and sound decisions.

Moreover, clear thinking entails much more than the act of thinking itself; it involves mental nurturing, health, and the shaping of our lives. Our thinking or thoughts essentially determines who we turn out to be. Every day you make varied decisions with far-reaching consequences, all from the same source—the mind. For good decisions, mental clarity and health are core. Clear thinking needs clear thoughts. A mind that is cluttered is on edge and distracted, and very little is achieved when your mind is not focused.

There is a lot that goes on in someone's brain. For that reason, you do not need to store everything in your brain. Get a tool that will help you write everything down. This should be like a storage gadget to put down any piece of information that you do not want to forget. For example, if you have an appointment or any future projects, have it diarized, or mark your calendar. You may also keep a journal, which is more detailed. A journal will help you offload anything that keeps you from getting things done, like relationship problems, giving you peace of mind.

Memories that are filled with the mistakes done, people we have wronged, past failures, and opportunities missed should be let go. Most people usually hold on to these memories and refuse to move past them. Memories that bring you down litter your mind and your life and cloud your mind from clear thinking.

When you decide to take on tasks, start by choosing the important one and work down the list until the last is tackled. Do not take on more than one task at a go. You then devote a specific amount of time to organize everything. During that time, ensure that your mind is clear, and push everything aside that can distract you from the task at hand.

Too much information can choke up your brain. This information that you take in every day, from reading magazines, newspapers, watching TV, accessing social media sites, and of course, surfing the web, must be controlled. You can limit the amount of information by setting the time you will spend on social media and other sources. Unsubscribe from online magazines and blogs that do not add any value to your life. Take opinions from individuals you hold in high regard, and finally, ignore information that is irrelevant.

Have a routine for every aspect of your life and everything you do. This will help reduce the stress your brain has to take. Even the minutiae—like what to eat for breakfast, lunch, and supper and what to wear every day—need to be scheduled and prepared in advance.

There are so many things that you need to do daily.

However, you cannot do everything. Have a list of things that are most important and deal with them. It leaves your mind time and space for mental clarity.

Mental clutter leads to obstruction of our inner thoughts and gets in the way of clear thinking and what is really important. Begin clearing your mind of all the unnecessary things that take up space in your mind but do not add any value or enhance clear thinking.

Personal change must first take place at the subconscious level; otherwise, it will never happen. Changing the way we think is the key to changing our lives and getting what we want or desire. Working on the subconscious to create a change of the mindset is as simple as planting the idea of what you want in your mind and intensely concentrating on it some time.

By working on the subconscious, you will highly likely release the latent power of your subconscious mind and come out with ways to get what you want within the time you give yourself. You are supposed to attract things, not run after them, and the subconscious mind is the key to get it to work.

Thank you once again for downloading this book, and I wish you a harmonious, happy, and fulfilling life free of anxiety. Please leave a good review and refer family, friends, relatives, and colleagues.

Are you happy with your life right now? What would make you happy? Do you have a plan for getting it?

Would you like some help? I might be able to help you. Are you be interested? Sign up for my newsletter. I give out a free workbook to help with social anxiety issues so those who sign up. I am also writing more books and posting articles that can help deal with other issues related to social anxiety. There's also a community that I'm building for people who are going through similar issues as you. If it's okay with you, I'd also like to get your feedback so I can write more about things that could help you. Does that sound like something that might help you? I hope it does, because I really want to help. I have been in your shoes before so I know how it feels. Join my newsletter and let's all help each other. Does that sound good? Visit my website now at **http://jen.green** and join my newsletter!

Made in the USA
Middletown, DE
16 March 2019